D1721941

THE SOUTH VIETNAM PEOPLE
WILL WIN

GENERAL VO NGUYEN GIAP

THE SOUTH VIETNAM PEOPLE WILL WIN

University Press of the Pacific
Honolulu, Hawaii

The South Vietnam People Will Win

by
General Vo Nguyen Giap

ISBN:0-89875-463-1

Reprinted from the 1965 edition

University Press of the Pacific
Honolulu, Hawaii
http://www.universitypressofthepacific.com

CONTENTS

THE LIBERATION WAR
OF THE SOUTH VIETNAM PEOPLE
AGAINST THE U.S. IMPERIALISTS
AND THEIR HENCHMEN
WILL CERTAINLY WIN *

---

* Article published in the **Nhan Dan** paper of July 19, 1964, on the occasion of the 10th anniversary of the signing of the Geneva Agreements on Indo-China (July 20, 1954).

Ten years ago on July 20, 1954, following the great victory of our army and people on the Dien Bien Phu battlefield, the Geneva Agreements were signed, restoring peace in Indo-China, on the basis of respect for the sovereignty, independence, unity and territorial integrity of our country, Vietnam, and of two friendly countries, Cambodia and Laos.

As laid down in the agreement, free general elections should be held throughout Vietnam two years after the armistice for the peaceful reunification of our country. To create every favourable condition for this work, the belligerent armies were provisionally regrouped respectively north and south of the 17th parallel and the administration of each zone undertook to ensure all democratic liberties for the people, at the same time not to accept weapons and military personnel from any country nor join any military alliance.

Ten years have elapsed since the Geneva Agreements were signed. During these ten years our people have successfully carried out socialist revolution and construction in the completely liberated North.

However, throughout these ten years the U.S imperialists and their henchmen have done their utmost to sabotage the Geneva Agreements and unleashed a war to invade and sell out the south of our country Thus, after fighting valiantly for ten years, making a great contribution to the victory of the first sacred resistance, our 14 million southern compatriots had again to rise up and wage a second sacred resistance against the U.S. imperialists and their stooges for independence, democracy, peace, neutrality, for the implementation of the Geneva Agreements and then for the reunification of the Fatherland.

On the occasion of the tenth anniversary of the signing of the Geneva Agreements on Indo-China, and as the struggle for national reunification of our people throughout the country is ten years old, let us review the revolutionary path fraught with perilous obstacles but full of glorious successes of our people, and assess the situation, the great achievements scored as well as the impending heavy tasks, the difficulties as well as the factors of certain victory, in order to heighten further our hatred for the enemy and the confidence in the victory, the grim determination and iron will of the heroic Vietnamese nation resolute to overcome all difficulties and obstacles, to confront any sacrifice and hardship, to fight, to march forward, to shatter all schemes of the U.S. imperialists and their henchmen and secure final victory.

I

The Geneva Agreements were a great victory of our people, the fruit of ten years of long and hard resistance, of nearly 100 years of national liberation struggle. This victory has safeguarded the gains of the August Revolution in the north of our country. It has helped the Vietnamese revolution in the North attain the socialist stage and the Democratic Republic of Vietnam become the first socialist country in South-East Asia.

For French and American imperialisms the Geneva Agreements were a most pitiful setback. They have put an end to the domination of the French colonialists in Indo-China. They have foiled the scheme of the U.S. imperialists to prolong and extend the war and turn the Indo-Chinese countries into U.S. new colonies and military bases. They were the bitterest defeat of the U.S. imperialists in South-East Asia after their disaster in the Chinese mainland and in Korea.

While the Indo-Chinese countries scored a great victory in their valiant and hard resistance and the

French Expeditionary Corps faced a grave danger U.S. imperialism made strenuous efforts to salvage the situation, but in the end it was forced together with its defeated ally to sit for negotiation to end the war. This came as no surprise to us and historical facts have given added proof that even when negotiating to reach an agreement, U S. imperialism already schemed to sabotage it with a view to impairing the victories of the Indo-Chinese peoples and restricting its defeats to the utmost.

No sooner had the ink of the signatures on the Geneva Agreements dried than the U.S. imperialists set up the aggressive South-East Asia military bloc and brazenly put South Vietnam, Cambodia and Laos under its protection. They schemed 'to consolidate further their strategic positions in South-East Asia while using this new aggressive bloc as a tool to carry on their war policy and curb the development of the national-liberation movement. *At utter variance with the provisions of the Geneva Agreements they plotted to continue their aggressive policy under the form of neo-colonialism with a view to turning South Vietnam, Cambodia and Laos into their new-type colonies and military bases.* This dark and perfidious scheme came out clearly in the statements of the U.S. Government that the security of the U S.A. was decided along the 17th parallel and the Vietnam-Laos border.

In the new strategic plan of the U.S. imperialists South Vietnam holds a position of utmost importance. This is precisely why soon after the armistice the

U.S A stopped all military aid to the French in Indo-China, ousted the latter from the South and rigged up the Ngo Dinh Diem administration entirely at its beck and call, hoping to use this subservient clique to suppress our compatriots' patriotic struggle in the South, rapidly *turn the South into a U.S. new-type colony and military base, and permanently partition our country.*

The U.S imperialists have trampled upon all the provisions of the Geneva Agreements, overtly introduced weapons, munitions and war material into the South at an accelerated tempo and increased their military personnel from 200 at the end of the war to 3,500 in 1961. They have frenziedly stepped up their intervention in every field, feverishly built up a regular and modern army for the puppet administration and strengthened such other anti-revolutionary armed forces as civil guard, people's militia, police and public security. They have frantically built up and extended military bases in the South and constructed a complete system of strategic roads so big and perfect as not only to cater for the aggressive war in South Vietnam but also to meet the greater requirements of the U S army in South-East Asia.

With the help of the U.S.imperialists, and in furtherance of their neo-colonialist policy, the Ngo Dinh Diem dethroned Bao Dai, a puppet of the French colonialists, illegally founded in the South the so-called Republic of Vietnam and resorted to oppression and coaxing to carry out separatist general elections, meanwhile they sealed off the provisional military demarcation line and turned down every proposal to re-establish normal relations and convene a consultative conference with the North.

Despite its signboard of "independence" and "democracy", its other deceptive policies such as "land reform", "rehabilitation of the national economy", since its very inception the Ngo Dinh Diem administration revealed itself as a traitorous clique and came up against a powerful opposition from all our compatriots in the South. It carried out a fascist dictatorial policy of utmost barbarity, launched hundreds of mopping-up campaigns with its regular army, perpetrated countless crimes and set up prisons everywhere to jail and torture patriots. It implemented a state policy of "indictment of communists" and "extermination of communists" to repress the former Resistance members, the parents of those regrouped in the North, those who stood for independence, freedom, peaceful national reunification and the implementation of the Geneva Agreements. It exterminated Buddhist, Cao Dai and Hoa Hao believers, and even terrorized those who had closely co-operated with it once they did not submit unconditionally.

This *unilateral war* started in 1954 became most atrocious in 1957-1959 after the U.S.-Diem clique had provisionally consolidated their administrative and military machine. The Phu Loi massacre and the law 10/1959 were typical of this most savage policy of terror. With their special military courts, prisons, guillotines and war-time repressive measures they hoped to drown in blood the patriotic movement of our southern compatriots in a short period, consolidate their selfish privileges and interests, and realize their dream of "pacifying the South, filling up the Ben Hai river and marching to the North".

However, far from yielding the expected results, the U.S.-Diem policy of war and terrorism roused a high indignation among all strata of our compatriots in the South. *Our fellow-countrymen held aloft the banner of peace, independence, reunification, democracy, and waged a persistent and valiant political struggle against the enemy, relying on the just cause and legality of the Geneva Agreements.*

When the U.S-Diem clique treacherously sabotaged the Geneva Agreements, everywhere meetings and demonstrations broke out, slogans appeared demanding an end to terror and reprisals, the re-establishment of North-South relations, a consultative conference for general elections, and the peaceful reunification of the country. The political struggle grew all the more powerful when the U.S. Diem clique resorted to such wily farces to sabotage further independence and national reunification as referendum and separatist general elections. It became fierce and bloody in the waves of struggle against the policy of "indictment of communists", the mopping-up operations and the massacres of the population. This unyielding political struggle, often waged in front of the muzzles or enemy guns, succeeded in checking and foiling part of their machiavellian schemes ; it highlighted our compatriots' indomitable spirit, frustrated the enemy's policy of "indictment and extermination of communists" which it had raised to the level of "state policy" in order to divide the southern people, liquidate patriots and quench the revolutionary movement. With various forms of struggle, relying on arguments, the legality of the Geneva Agreements and the pressure of the masses, our compatriots showed their patriotism and solidarity in struggle, exposed the dictatorial and traitorous Ngo Dinh Diem administration, drove it into ever growing isolation and pilloried it.

Throughout five years of arduous and fierce political struggle with their bare hands against the violence of the enemy, our southern compatriots experienced countless sufferings and losses but they carried the day.

Thousands of villages were burnt by the enemy and hundreds of thousands of people jailed, tortured and killed in prisons and concentration camps. But sufferings and losses could not damp our people's combativeness and patriotism. On the contrary, through their fierce political struggle, our compatriots were tempered and become aware of the ferocity of the U.S.-Diem clique, of its irremediable fundamental weakness for it is the enemy of the people and of the fatherland, for it represents violence and injustice.

Through their fierce political struggle, our compatriots clearly realized that *to overthrow the enemy, attain the fundamental aspirations of the broad masses of the people there was no other way than wage a revolutionary struggle.* Far from quenching our compatriots' revolutionary spirit, U.S -Diem guns, bullets, prisons, re-education centres and fascist laws exacerbated it all the more. For five years on end the U.S.-Diem clique waged a real war against the people, but the latter's revolutionary spirit hold out and in many vast areas the revolutionary forces were still kept intact.

*

* *

The end of 1959 and beginning of 1960 marked a *new development* in the southern revolutionary movement. *The persistent political struggle in the past years now bolstered by an armed struggle for self-defence, grew all the more powerful and sweeping.* The revolutionary mettle of the masses in the Mekong delta as well as in the immense Western Highlands rose as an overflowing tide. The enemy's grip was broken over vast areas, in some places the enemy grass-root administration was disintegrated, the cruel devils isolated or punished, the prosperity zones were destroyed, nearly 80 per cent of their inhabitants liberated. *The political situation of the U.S.-Diem administration underwent a serious and endless crisis.* In face of the people's new revolutionary high tide, they realized that their scheme to "pacify" the South rapidly and use it as a base to attack the North was obviously a fiasco ; they had to devote all their efforts to deal with the new developments of the movement.

The U.S. imperialists openly stepped up their armed intervention in the south of our country. In May 1961 the *bilateral military agreement* between U.S. Vice-

President Johnson and Ngo Dinh Diem was signed, then come into being *the Staley-Taylor plan* and the setting up of the U.S. Military Command in Saigon under Gen. Paul Harkins. *The U.S. imperialists and their henchmen decided to launch an "undeclared war" in the South, to use this area as a testing ground for their so-called "special war" aimed at repressing the national liberation movement.*

In brief the plan of this "special war", the Staley-Taylor plan, envisaged three stages : first, to "pacify" the South and establish a network of spy-commando centres in the North ; then to rehabilitate the economy, increase the puppet military forces in the South while stepping up sabotage work in the North ; lastly to develop the southern economy and to attack the North.

To carry out the first stage regarded as most important they worked out a series of new measures among which the increase of the army's effectives, the improvement of the equipment and the raising of the fighting capacities of the puppet armed forces as well as the enforcement of the "state policy" of "strategic hamlets" aimed at gradually concentrating and controlling the bulk of the population. The U.S. imperialists stepped up their multiform aid to the Ngo Dinh Diem administration, first of all the military aid. They reckoned that within 18 months viz. by the end of 1962, the superincreased reactionary military forces would certainly smash the people's political and military revolutionary forces : meanwhile most of the 14 million of our compatriots in the South would be herded into "strategic hamlets", kept under close watch and severed from all connections with the guerilla groups : the whole of South Vietnam would then be "pacified" ; their first stage would be brought to completion.

At the outset the enemy's perfidious scheme did cause new difficulties to our compatriots in the South. However, inspired with an unshakable determination to struggle and a dogged will to overthrow the enemy of the nation, our compatriots have carried on their valiant struggle in order to frustrate the U.S. imperialists' new plan of armed intervention. *To oppose the U.S.-Diem "special war" the southern people have launched a sweeping and powerful guerilla war, an all-out and protracted people's resistance.* At the beginning our compatriots in the South had only their bare hands while the enemy had a marked superiority in material forces. Our people in the South had to put up an extremely hard and fierce struggle, opposing justice to aggression, weakness to strength, heroism to modern weapons. Capturing enemy weapons to equip themselves our army and people in the South have overcome all difficulties and trials, develop their forces rapidly, scored success after success and will win ever greater victories.

The U.S.-Diem clique regarded the military measure as most efficient to crush our armed forces and political bases. Throughout 1962 and 1963 our army and people inflicted upon them many military setbacks. Unable to bring out the expected results, the "helicopter tactics", modern weapons, chemical poisons, etc. could not even save their authors from bitter failures. Most of the raids, big and small, upon the villages were repelled or smashed The southern army and people annihilated many enemy posts, stormed many enemy garrisons, attacked reinforcements or convoys on road and on water. Early in 1963 the resounding Ap Bac victory of the Liberation army and My Tho guerillas highlighted our fighters' boundless heroism and created a seething emulation movement to kill the enemy and score exploits throughout the patriotic armed forces in the South. According to the figures released by the Liberation News Agency, in three years of guerilla warfare (1961-1963) our southern army and people destroyed and put out of action more than 250,000 enemy troops among them nearly 1,500 Americans, shot down and damaged hundreds of enemy planes, captured over 30,000 weapons of all kinds.

The state policy of strategic hamlets is the backbone of the "special war"; the U.S.-Diem clique pinned all their hopes on this policy and mustered manpower and wealth to enforce it at any cost. They reckoned that in a short time they could build 17,000 "strategic hamlets", turning the South into a huge system of prisons. However, at the very start, their plan met with our compatriots' fierce opposition. The herding of people was not easy as they expected, the tempo of building "strategic hamlets" was slowed down as time passed. A number of "strategic hamlets" were destroyed immediately after their establishment or so many times that the enemy could not consolidate them. Others once destroyed were turned into fighting villages, solid strongholds for guerilla warfare. The highest figure of hamlets set up fell short of 6,000/7,000 according to the very statistics of the Ngo Dinh Diem administration.

Together and in co-ordination with the military struggle and destruction of "strategic hamlets" there developed a sweeping and powerful political struggle involving all strata of the people. Many a time the political force of the masses crushed enemy mopping-up operations and successfully protected our compatriots' lives and property. It is this same force that destroyed the rural administration bloc after bloc, liberated many vast areas in the countryside and called upon tens of thousands of enemy troops and officials to cross over to the people's side. In 1962-1963 alone, more than 50 million individual participations in political struggles under various forms and sizes were recorded. The seething struggle during the second half of 1963 put up by the Buddhist believers, youths, students, intellectuals and labouring people in the towns, big and small, especially in Hue and Saigon - Cholon plunged the U.S.-Diem clique into an ever deeper crisis.

After two years of large-scale "special war" the U.S. imperialists and their henchmen faced many difficulties and setbacks both in the military and political fields. The time limit of 18 months having elapsed, *their strategy of rapid "pacification" of the South once again floundered. The Staley-Taylor plan turned out to be a fiasco* in face of the boundless heroism of our army and people in the South.

*

* *

Owing to the repeated defeats of the "special war", the internal contradictions between the U.S. imperialists and their henchmen grew so sharp that late in 1963 and early in 1964, the U.S. imperialists had to stage two coups d'état aimed at swapping horses midstream and salvaging the situation. Ngo Dinh Diem and Ngo Dinh Nhu were overthrown and assassinated; soon after that the Duong Van Minh clique was also replaced by new henchmen, the Khanh-Hoan clique.

Throughout nine years, the Diem-Nhu brothers efficiently served the U.S. imperialists, sold out their country and their compatriots, and were praised by the Americans as "anti-communist fighters number one" in South-East Asia, "great men" of the "free world". Now, forced to overthrow Diem-Nhu and ready to kill their faithful servants, the U.S. imperialists avowed the shameful failure of their policy of new-type colony, the fiasco of their so-called "special war". The pitiful collapse of Diem-Nhu threw consternation into the ranks of the puppet administration and army, roused bewilderment and weariness among them. It could not solve the ever sharper contradictions between the U.S. imperialists and their henchmen, and instead rendered them more acute and complicated. It could not bolster the sagging morale of the puppet troops and officials, and shattered it still.

Late in 1963 and particularly early in 1964 our people in the South made the best use of the enemy's weak points and difficulties, stepped up their activities in every field, and scored great victories. According to the preliminary statistics of the Liberation News Agency, in the first six months of this year the southern army and people fought nearly 14,000 battles, razed to the ground 400 enemy posts, smashed and forced the enemy to withdraw from over 550 other posts, annihilated and captured 42,000 enemy troops, among them more than 500 Americans, put out of action nearly 30,000 of them, seized 5,000 weapons of all kinds, millions of bullets and hand grenades, shot down 170 planes of various types, damaged over 320 others. Our people from the Nam Bo delta and the Western Highlands to the Fifth Zone coastal areas rose up and demolished nearly 2,000 "strategic hamlets", extended the liberated zone in many regions. The above figures prove that *the southern resistance is entering a new stage and the balance of forces is continuously tipping in our favour.*

Of course, in face of this situation, with their extremely reactionary and cruel nature the U.S. imperialists do not admit themselves beaten but frenziedly stepped up their aggressive war. Now they have to envisage a protracted war in the South. They work out a new strategic plan, the *Johnson-McNamara plan* aimed at "pacifying" the South within 1964-1965. This new plan does not basically differ from the bankrupt Staley-Taylor plan. What is new is that the U.S. imperialists make greater efforts to increase their war means in the hope of securing better results for their special war. The puppet armed forces are brought to 350,000 regular troops, apart from 200,000 civil guards and reactionary fighting youths; the number of U.S. advisers and servicemen now reach 25,000; aircraft

of all types amount to over 700 ; all other weapons a
also increased. The military aid for 1964 goes up frc
500 to 625 million dollars. This is a fairly great w
effort by the U.S. imperialists aimed at salvaging t
desperate situation of the puppet army, mustering
forces to "pacify" according to plan the areas controlled by the guerillas, first of all again to tighten
their grip on the eight provinces in the Mekong delta
and a number of regions in South Trung Bo.

To achieve the above new plan, the U.S. imperialists
sent Gen. Taylor, Chairman of the U.S. Joint Chiefs
of staff as Ambassador to the South. This appointment
of Taylor shows that the U.S. imperialists are most
obdurate and cling to their "big stick foreign policy"'
which has met with failure these past ten years in the
South. Taylor is the very man who advocated the
theory on "special war" which has been tested for the
first time in the South and obviously gone bankrupt
Taylor is also the exponent of the theory of pacification
of the South within 18 months, however twice 18
months have elapsed and this plan has not yet been
initially carried out and has been replaced by a new
one. The appointment of Taylor to South Vietnam
recalls us of that of such best French generals as De
Tassigny and Navarre to Indo-China every time the
French Expeditionary Corps was in serious difficulty.
Our compatriots in the South and the heroic Southern
Liberation troops though having to fight a protracted
and hard war will certainly reserve Taylor or any
U.S. aggressive general the fate our people reserved
to the former defeated French generals.

II

Over the past ten years, the fierce struggle between the enemy and us has developed as follows :

On the enemy side, with a view to transforming South Vietnam into a U.S. military base and colony, the U.S. imperialists and their henchmen have followed a policy of terrorism and repression, carried on for several years a unilateral war and afterwards a large-scale "special war" in which U.S. armed intervention has been intensified day by day.

On our side, in order to realize the fundamental aspirations of our people : peace, independence, democracy, and progress towards national reunification, our southern compatriots have waged for several years a political struggle, and afterwards by means of political violence and armed forces, started a sacred patriotic resistance against the enemy "special war".

Over the past ten years, *the South Vietnam society* has undergone thorough-going and important changes.

Throughout the French rule, the southern Vietnam society like the rest of our country, was a *colonial and semi-feudal* one. After the successful August

Revolution, the Democratic Republic of Vietnam made its appearance. With the reconquest by the French colonialists' troops, part of our country *bore the character of a people's democracy while part of it remained a colonial and semi-feudal country.* Our entire people's great Resistance War ended with the historic Dien Bien Phu victory. On the basis of the Geneva Agreements and due to the U.S. imperialists' intervention in South Vietnam, our country has been temporarily divided into two zones with differing politico-social systems. The North completely liberated, has been successfully building socialism while the South becoming a U.S. new-type colony, has borne the character of a colonial and semi-feudal society. After ten years of revolutionary struggle, new changes in line with the upward trend of history have taken place : Today part of South Vietnam *remains colonial and semi-feudal while part of it, viz. the ever enlarged free zone, bears a new character :* there our compatriots enjoy independence, democracy and freedom.

The very nature of such a society has shown that at present in South Vietnam there exist *two fundamental contradictions: one* between our southern people and the aggressive imperialists, first of all the U.S. imperialists and their henchmen ; *the other* is the contradiction between the southern people, first of all the peasants, and feudal landlordism. These contradictions have defined i) the character of the revolution in the South which is a *national democratic revolution ; ii)* its strategic task which is the overthrow of imperialism, the completion of national independence in combination with the overthrow of feudal-landlordism, and the completion of people's democracy.

Due to the collusion between U.S. imperialism and the local reactionary forces, the South Vietnam society is bearing a main contradiction, between our southern people on the one hand and aggressive imperialism and its lackeys representative of the most reactionary pro-American feudal-landlords and compradore bourgeois on the other. This main contradiction defines the *concrete object and immediate task of the revolution* in South Vietnam, as well as the organization of forces for the completion of this revolutionary task.

At present all our southern compatriots, broadly and closely united, are waging a patriotic war to overthrow U.S. imperialism and the puppet administration. A detailed analysis must be made of the characteristics of this war, the understanding of which will enable us to grasp the character, objective and law of development of our liberation war. This understanding is obviously related to the formulation of a correct leading line which will take our liberation war to final victory.

Characteristics of the enemy

The object of the present liberation war in the South *is neo-colonialism of U.S. imperialism and its lackeys. These are an ultra-reactionary and ruthless enemy materially strong in many points, but very weak morally and politically.*

Soon after the restoration of peace in Indo-China, the object of the revolution in South Vietnam has changed. American imperialism has kicked out defeated French colonialism, seized South Vietnam and established the pro-American Ngo Dinh Diem administration. U.S. imperialism has neither settled a ruling machinery nor utilized occupation troops in the South as French old colonialism did ; but through interventionist policies, and military and economic aid, it has controlled the South in all fields.

Neo-colonialism which is being practised by American imperialism in South Vietnam, is a product of imperialism in modern times. Due to the growing influence of the world socialist system, and the national-liberation movement which is storming in many countries of Asia, Africa and Latin America, the imperialists can no longer rule over their colonies with old methods while the native reactionary forces also are frightened and anxious for their privileges. *Neo-colonialism is precisely the collusion and compromise between foreign imperialists and a section of native compradore bourgeois and reactionary feudal-landlords to maintain the colonial rule under new forms and methods, while checking and opposing the movement of the broad masses.*

Neo-colonialism is by nature a concentrated expression of the basic tendency of capitalism : enslavement of weak and small nations, search and wrangle about markets and raw materials, utter oppression and exploitation of the people of these nations. Its main practice is reliance on violence. It differs from old colonialism in the fact that *it carries out its policy of enslavement and uses violence not directly, but indirectly* by the medium of a puppet administration and army vested with sham independence and democracy, and in the form of "aid" or "alliance" in all respects. Neo-colonialism screens its aggressive and exploiting nature in all clothings, therefore it is all the more cunning and wicked, and easily induces the peoples to relax their vigilance. In the South, after the defeat of French imperialism, old colonialism was completely doomed and was buried together with the images of its cruel or crafty governor generals and high commissioners and its ruthless expeditionary corps against the will of U.S. imperialism which, unable to revive that decaying corpse, is compelled to act under the cloak of neo-colonialism.

Neo-colonialism relies on its quislings as a tool to carry out its policy. Its strength is drawn partly from the vast economic and military possibilities — which are many — of the metropolis, but on the other hand, is directly determined by the fact that whether or not the native reactionary forces are strong economically and politically. In South Vietnam, the U.S. sponsored puppet administration was set up at a time when our people were gaining successes and imperialism meeting with failure, therefore right from its inception, it lacked vitality and was fraught with the predisposing causes of inner contradictions, crises and wars Its social basis is next to nil : feudalism, landlordism and compradore bourgeoisie which had not been very strong under the French rule, were weakened and differentiated during the years of Resistance war. After the restoration of peace, they were again divided due to the contradictions between the U.S.A. and France. On the contrary, the revolutionary people have reached a very high degree of political consciousness, and are united into a very great strength.

In these conditions, the U.S. backed puppet administration cannot stand firm on its feet without closely clinging to its bosses and making themselves docile lackeys at the beck and call of U.S. imperialism in all affairs big or small. In face of the people's revolutionary high tide, it is compelled to embark rapidly in dictatorship and fascism, feverishly carrying out the U.S. policy of military intensification, and war preparation. For its own existence, it is forced to declare bluntly its opposition to the Geneva Agreements and the dear aspirations of our people, viz, peace, independence, democracy and national reunification. That is why, despite the U.S.-Diem slogans of "overthrowing colonialism", "boycotting feudalism", "extermination of communists" and their boastful claim of liquidating social evils or carrying out a number of demagogic reforms, the large masses of people have immediately made out behind the mended cloak the real face of the international gendarme which is U.S. imperialism, and that of the Ngo family which for many generations, have served as running dogs, and are all the more resolute in their struggle against them. For many years, the U.S. backed puppet administration has had to resort to a policy of violence in order to repress the movement, using privileges and interests as a lure to create a new generation of traitors ; strive to put under its close control the army, the police and the administration at various levels in an attempt to enlarge its social bases. But the rising tide of the ever-sweeping and powerful struggle of our people, coupled with the coup d'état overthrowing the rule of the Ngo family has inflicted heavy losses upon U.S. imperialism; the rank of its quislings can no more be consolidated, let alone enlarged

The policy of U.S. imperialism and its henchmen is one of invasion and selling out South Vietnam. In consequence both the unilateral war they started in 1954 and the special war they have kindled recently are only aimed at repressing the people's revolutionary movement, dominating and enslaving South Vietnam and transforming it into a U.S. neo-colony and military base. This is clearly *an unjust war, an aggressive war*. Therefore, in consideration of its political goal and nature, the war carried on by U.S. imperialism and its henchmen is by no means different from the aggressive war kindled by French colonialism in former times to enslave our people once more.

In the U.S. imperialists' strategy of "flexible response", "special war" ranks third, coming after world nuclear war and limited war. In consideration of the balance of world forces tipping unfavourably to them, and the immediate difficulties met in the kindling of a large-scale war, the U.S. imperialists hope to win successes in "limited war" with conventional weapons, especially in the "special wars" aimed at repressing the liberation movement of the weak and small nations. U.S. brasshats have made a thorough-going study of the characteristics of this kind of war the aim of which, in their opinion is to oppose guerilla war, that is the people's war, therefore special warfare takes place within the limit of a country with no fixed frontline and rare mobilization of large-units; on the other hand, there must be an all-round combination of military, political, psychological and economic activities. The foregoing features regarding the limit, scale or real characteristics of special war by no means change its nature: *special war is aggressive war*.

U.S. imperialism, the sworn enemy of the southern people and of our entire nation, possessed of a capitalist economy with most developed modern industry, is the most barbarous imperialist chieftain, the main force of war and aggression, the bulwark of the world counter-revolutionary forces. Economically and militarily it is a strong enemy.

Compared with French imperialism in former times, it has greater possibilities in all respects, in money and in modern weapons which are stockpiled in great quantities. But the assessment we make of the enemy forces must be factual. We must view them not only on the basis of the balance of world forces in general, but also within the limit of a given area, within the real limit of the southern part of our country. Today in the world, the U.S. military and economic forces are still strong, but compared with the revolutionary forces which are developing throughout the world, they are in a weaker position than before. Moreover, U.S. imperialism is being attacked on all sides, and has to scatter its forces in many places.

It suffered heavy defeats in China, Korea, Cuba, is being beaten in Laos, South Vietnam, and meeting with difficulties in many other places.

Today in South Vietnam the U.S. imperialists and their lackeys are ever more isolated politically. Militarily speaking, their army is superior to ours in effectives, modern weapons and mobility. All their temporarily strong points must be studied carefully especially when solving the questions regarding operations and campaigns. However, it is certain that all these strong points cannot make up for their most basic weak points in morale and politics, which are inherent in an enemy of the people, in a counter-revolutionary army. But in the south of our country, these weak points are all the more serious due to weakness of the southern reactionary forces, and the pecular form of the aggressive war which is taking place there.

a) Either in the unilateral war in former times or in the special war at present, the U.S. imperialists and their lackeys have been conducting an unjust war, that of aggressors and traitors trampling under foot the most elementary rights of our people, and the dearest aspirations of our nation. Therefore, they are meeting with the fierce resistance of our 14 million southern compatriots. They are fighting a whole nation.

b) In this "special war" their military forces are mainly the puppet army. But the absolute majority of their men being sons of the toiling people, cannot find it in their hearts to go on serving as cannon fodder to defend the interests of the enemy. In face of the fierce struggle and successes of the people and Liberation Army, the hatred for war will certainly develop among the reactionary troops. An evergrowing number of soldiers stirred by patriotism will certainly turn their guns against the enemy and side with the people. Moreover, due to the weakening of the social basis of the reactionary forces as a result of their inner contradictions which have grown acute and intricate, the enemy has less and less conditions to consolidate his army and administration ; the morale of the officials in the puppet administration and of the men among the puppet army is flagging markedly with every passing day.

c) To consolidate the reactionary army, the U.S. imperialists bring in more advisers, military personnel and even several task forces. The introduction of greater U.S. military forces into South Vietnam is immediately effective in controlling the reactionary military forces of their henchmen more closely. But we must clearly realize that for the U.S.A., the introduction of more military forces into South Vietnam is politically a most passive action. The increase of American military forces will diminish the "special" character of the war. The new face of colonialism has become more ineffective. Our people's hatred will increase, the contradiction between the U.S. advisers and the puppet officers and men will be sharpened, not to mention the weakness of the G.I.s in a war against the guerillas in a tropical battlefield such as South Vietnam. Even U.S. brasshats have to recognize that these weak points have greatly curtailed the effectiveness of their activities.

Our characteristics

Our southern people, the brass wall of the Fatherland, are conducting a liberation war against a new-style aggressive war kindled by the U.S. imperialists for independence, democracy, peace and neutrality in view of achieving national reunification *Compared with the enemy's force our people's force is for the time being much weaker materially, but on the contrary, it is very strong politically and morally.*

The South like the rest of Vietnam was a colonial and semi-feudal country with an extremely backward economy which was moreover ruined by war for many years. After the restoration of peace, it has not yet time to bring its production to normal when it again fell victim to another aggressive war. Our southern people have had to endure privations and misery caused by a war dragging out for decades. With the successful August Revolution the people's power was established. This power was afterwards maintained and consolidated in the free zones, guerilla zones and guerilla bases throughout the years of nation-wide resistance ; however, implementing the Geneva Agreements, our power gradually gave place to that of the reactionaries, henchmen of the U.S. imperialists.

For the same reason our people's armed forces in South Vietnam, which had matured on the Fifth zone and Mekong delta battlefields during the years of Resistance against the French, regrouped to the North, provisionally leaving behind their beloved native land which they had protected at the cost of their blood, while on their part tens of thousands of enemy troops withdrew from the Bac Bo delta. Not only our guerilla bases and guerilla zones ceased to exist, but even our immense free zones are temporarily put under the control of the opponents. Availing themselves of these conditions, the U.S. imperialists and the Ngo Dinh Diem administration started a unilateral war to extinguish the patriotic movement with a view to transforming South Vietnam into an American new-type colony and military base. They pinned their hope on our ruined economy and on the very difficult conditions created by the absence of a people's power and army to protect them. And they thought that our southern people had no other way than letting themselves subjugated by their bayonets and guillotines.

But our southern compatriots are really a heroic people. *They are possessed of an invincible potential power* and a political strength which the U.S. imperialists and their quislings are incapable to understand. They have coped with a people having a very high revolutionary spirit and very great political superiority. Revolutionary theory is translated into invincible strength once it has gripped the masses. In a revolutionary war, the people's political superiority will be translated into a material force capable of turning the table on the enemy, overcoming all difficulties and hardships to defeat in the end an enemy who at first was several times stronger. The southern people are indeed outstanding sons of the Vietnamese people, a people having the tradition of struggling to the bitter end against foreign invasion, "rather to sacrifice their lives than be enslaved". Our southern people made the Nam Ky and Ba To insurrections, in the historic days of August they rose up to take the revolution to victory and establish the people's power, they enjoyed the political and economic rights brought to them by the revolution, and fought heroically, making an important contribution to the victory of the great Resistance war of the nation. After a long revolutionary struggle the southern people reached a high political and organizational level, gained many experiences from their political and their armed struggles. For this reason, in face of a most barbarous enemy, the revolutionary movement in the South has been maintained and developed with every passing day.

The southern people armed with a revolutionary spirit and the experiences gained in their revolutionary struggle, are moreover encouraged by the strength of a just cause and closely sealed into a very strong and firm bloc by *lofty revolutionary goals:* national independence, land to the tillers, basic freedoms, peace and national reunification. After a national democratic revolutionary struggle fraught with sacrifice and hardships, and a great patriotic Resistance war, the lofty national democratic ideals broadly disseminated by the Party since 1930 have taken deep root into the heart and mind of the masses of people. We cannot give up fighting so long as we have not wrested back independence, land, and the basic rights to life. The national Resistance war ended successfully, the Geneva Agreements recognized Vietnam's sovereignty, independence, unity and territorial integrity; the battle cannot come to an end so long as these clauses of the agreements are not implemented. The southern people are determined to hold firm the national and democratic banner and raise it aloft till victory.

In the former Resistance years, President Ho Chi Minh used to say; *"unity, unity, and broad unity; victory, victory, and great victory."* The southern people clearly realize that unity is strength, unity is the main factor of victory. Though the enemy is materially strong, he is constantly divided by inner contradictions, while the southern people on the contrary enjoy a *tradition of broad unity* established throughout the first sacred Resistance war. In the first years following the restoration of peace, the struggle was fraught with difficulties and hardships, the southern patriots though at times severed from one another organizationally, are closely bound to one another morally. The love for one's own fellow-countrymen, the national pride and solidarity, and the pursuit of common revolutionary goals are sources of strength encouraging our compatriots firmly to maintain and actively to broaden unity. If the South Vietnam Liberation National Front has grown rapidly and enjoyed such a great prestige among the people, it is mainly due to the experiences gained in the past and the traditions of national unity, and to the development and application of these experiences to the new historical conditions.

Moreover, the southern people are encouraged to organize themselves along a *correct political line and in adequate forms of struggle.* For this reason, however atrocious the enemy, and however difficult and dangerous the conditions of struggle may be, the political and armed forces of the people are growing stronger and stronger. The process of revolutionary struggle of the southern people is a development from political struggle to armed struggle, and then both of them being combined with each other and enhancing each other. The southern people have developed to a high degree their political superiority, worked out a correct principle and a great many forms of struggle. Politically and militarily speaking the revolutionary struggle in the South has been developing to a fairly high degree thanks to the creative spirit of the masses ; it therefore has been able to thwart many dangerous policies and manœuvres of the enemy, frustrate his modern strategy and achieve greater and greater successes.

The revolutionary war waged by our compatriots in the South has been carried on when half of our country is liberated and advancing to socialism. *The North is a hope and an encouragement for the southern people, especially* in the years when the enemy carries out most atrocious terrorization and repression. Liberated North is a pride of the entire Vietnamese people, a firm and strong base of the struggle for national reunification. Our southern compatriots feel that their northern fellow-countrymen are always close by their side in the struggle against a common enemy, which enhances their confidence and strengthen their determination in overcoming all difficulties on their advance to victory.

Over the past years, our southern people have been struggling against a most barbarous enemy. The most reactionary and inhuman nature of the U.S. imperialists and their puppet administration have wrought havoc with our southern people who become all the more aware of the real face of the enemy of the nation and nurture an ever deeper hatred for him. In war the fighting spirit and hatred is a huge force. This explains why the U.S. jet helicopters, amphibious cars, ultra rapid sub-machineguns, flame throwers, automatic mines, noxious chemicals, unsinkable landing craft, and other U.S. modern weapons cannot save the puppet army from repeated failures.

On the contrary, the Southern liberation forces are armed only with rudimentary weapons, but their very high fighting spirit have helped them score success after success.

At present, the revolutionary war in the South is still facing many difficulties and hardships, however with their heroic fighting spirit, our southern compatriots and Liberation Army have scored great successes and created steady factors of strategical significance. The people's political forces and revolutionary armed forces have grown stronger and stronger, the liberated area wider. Our southern people are turning the table on the enemy, and the successful development of the liberation war in South Vietnam has eloquently testified that in a revolutionary struggle and in war, the decisive factor is in the last analysis, man and political lines and the decisive strength is that of the masses of people.

Characteristics of the international conditions

The "special war" kindled by the U.S. imperialists and their henchmen and the liberation war put up by our southern people takes place when the *international conditions are favourable to us and unfavourable to the enemy.*

Over the past ten years, the world has witnessed great revolutionary changes advantageous to the struggle for peace, national independence, democracy and socialism.

The world socialist system, though facing many difficulties, continues to grow stronger and stronger in all fields, unceasingly develop its role as a bulwark of world revolution, of the national liberation movement and world peace movement. Especially in Asia, Africa and Latin America, the national-liberation movement is developing far and wide, dealing telling blows to imperialism with U.S. imperialism in the lead. The workers' movement in capitalist countries and the peace movement are also rising high The van forces of this era are the international communist movement despite the serious differences of views now existing concerning the lines to follow ; however these differences, which are temporary, will certainly be removed by the reality of world revolution ; the rank of the genuine communists in the world will be cemented by a close unity and will grow by leaps and bounds in the struggle for the purity of Marxism-Leninism against modern revisionism. The balance of forces in the world shows that the revolutionary forces are stronger than the reactionary forces, the forces of peace are stronger than the forces of war. We are rising, the enemy is declining. These international conditions are basically favourable to the struggle for liberation of our southern people, and unfavourable to the aggressive "special war" kindled by the U.S. imperialists.

Lately, bogged down in South Vietnam, the U.S. imperialists had to call for help from their allies. But except for a number of impotent lackeys such as the ruling circles in Thailand, Taiwan, and South Korea who have voiced their support, most of the U.S. allies have given a token support or cold-shouldered the appeal. The French government declared its blunt disapproval for the U.S. continued armed intervention in Indo-China, and proposed the neutralization of the South-East Asian countries. A noteworthy fact is the indifference of many members of the SEATO and NATO: of late, the proposal made by the U.S. government asking the above-mentioned countries to give their contributions to sabotage the South Vietnam situation, has brought in no practical results. Formerly, in their predicament in Indo-China, the French Expeditionary Corps pinned their hopes on U.S. reinforcements. Today bogged down in South Vietnam, it is hard for the U.S. imperialists to expect an aid from their allies, because no one likes "to shed blood without receiving anything in return". And if in former times, while carrying on the aggressive war in Korea, the U.S. imperialists could gain the support of the majority of the U.N.O. members and the assistance of the great capitalist countries and a number of other countries, today in their "special war" in South Vietnam, *they are obviously more and more isolated,* being condemned not only by public world progressive opinion but even by their allies.

On our side, *our just liberation war has enjoyed the broadest sympathy and support in the world arena.* Not only are the peoples of the socialist countries, the peoples of the Soviet Union, China, and other fraternal countries, supporting us wholeheartedly, but the peoples of the nationalist countries, the progressive people all over the world also voice their solidarity. Our southern people have also enjoyed the warm support — moral and material — of the mass organizations as well as of many governments. Days of international solidarity with the South Vietnam people were organized everywhere. Since December 1961, more than 30 delegations of the South Vietnam Liberation National Front and of various patriotic organizations within the Front have visited 19 countries in Asia, Africa, Latin America and Europe. Many organizations within the Front have been affiliated to their international counterparts. Today, the South Vietnam Liberation National Front has its official standing representatives in Cuba, Algeria, Czechoslovakia, and the German Democratic Republic. Lately, the American people, including many intellectuals, outstanding personalities, priests, and a number of M.P. have also voiced their demand to put an end to the dirty war kindled by the U.S. government in South Vietnam. It can be said that in the international arena the heroic struggle of our southern compatriots has enjoyed a wide and strong sympathy and support ever known in the annals of our people's revolutionary struggle.

We must appreciate the sympathy and support of the world forces for peace, national independence, democracy and socialism in favour of the liberation struggle of our southern people and regard it as an important factor taking them to final victory.

On the other hand, compared with the first years of our National Resistance war, when our country was encircled on all sides, the Resistance war put up by our southern people at the present time is enjoying much more favourable conditions. The South is struggling not only when the North has been liberated, but also concurrently with the friendly neighbour countries. Laos is fighting heroically against the U.S. imperialists and their lackeys, and Cambodia is frustrating their dark design in order to defend her active neutrality. Moreover adjoined to the immense socialist camp, South Vietnam, regarded by the U.S. imperialists as an important link in their South-East Asian strategic chain, is at the same time the centre of the liberation movement of the nations opposing U.S. imperialism in this area. South-East Asia is also a regime in which the peoples have time and again risen up to wage a revolutionary struggle for self-liberation, under the leadership of the experienced Marxist-Leninist parties. This is an important encouragement for our compatriots in South Vietnam.

III

As has been said above, during the last ten years, in South Vietnam, the revolutionary struggle of our people has shifted from the political form to the form of political and armed struggle and has now become a national liberation war waged by the entire people against the "special war" unleashed by the U.S. imperialists and their lackeys.

Basing ourselves on the characteristics stated in part II, we can draw the conclusion that : *the war for liberation put up by the South Vietnam people at present is a nation-wide, all-sided, self-supporting, long-term and arduous war which in the end will certainly be victorious.* Besides this fundamental political content, similar to that of the former patriotic war against the French colonialists and American interventionists, the present war for liberation of our people in the South has its own pecularities in that our enemy is not the old-colonialism of the French imperialists but the neo-colonialism of the U.S. imperialists ; our southern compatriots have now made great progress in ideology and organization ; the international condition is more favourable, and also the form of warfare used by the enemy is the aggressive war of a special type and not of a classical one.

*
* *

It is clear that this is a *war waged by the entire people*. For the sake of safeguarding the vital interests of the nation, in face of the danger that their country is subjugated, their homes destroyed, their lives threatened and their property trampled under foot, fourteen million of our compatriots in the South, regardless of age, sex, nationality, creed and political affiliation, are resolved not to be enslaved and have risen together against the U.S. imperialists and their henchmen.

The war has been waged by the entire people because *the political goals of the war for liberation* are just and very lofty, the South Vietnam Liberation National Front has a correct political line which can mobilize and organize the entire people. The platform of the Front : "*To struggle for peace, neutrality, independence and democracy and for the future reunification of the country*" has reflected the primary and urgent requirements and the most profound aspirations of the South Vietnam people. It has satisfied the immediate revolutionary task created by the social condition of South Vietnam.

The U.S. imperialists have done their best to practise neo-colonialism, to set up the "Republic of Vietnam" having its "independence" and "sovereignty" because they want to overshadow the fundamental contradictions between our people and the aggressive imperialists, and to create conditions for the puppet administration hidden behind the false pattern of nation and sovereignty to deceive the masses and win over them. However, the Ngo Dinh Diem administration, owing to the conditions which originated it and to the policies it was compelled to follow from its inception, did not succeed in its deceit and laid bare its face of traitor to the country.

In face of the perfidious scheme of neo-colonialism and the puppet administration, we must raise all the higher the banner of *national independence*. That is why the slogan : national independence and the urgent clauses for national salvation put forth by the South Vietnam Liberation National Front have been able to broadly rally all patriotic and democratic forces in a united front against the imperialists and their stooges on the basis of the worker-peasant alliance. Not only the grass-root worker-peasant masses, but all the sections of petty-bourgeois intelligentsia, the national bourgeoisie and patriotic personalities have risen as one man against the common enemy under the banner of national independence. The minority people in the South have set a shining example of indomitable spirit. Most of the religious sects also approve of the Front's platform ; even the pro-French elements and the large majority of catholic refugees from the North, have today sympathized with the Front and taken part, to a certain degree, in the struggle for national salvation.

In a revolution to liberate a colonial or semi-colonial and semi-feudal country the anti-imperialist question cannot be taken apart from the anti-feudal question, nor can the national revolution be separated from the democratic revolution, because, the substance and content of the national question is the peasant question ; without putting forth the democratic question, without rousing the great peasant masses, it is quite impossible to consolidate and strengthen the national united front, and to set up a solid worker-peasant alliance which can serve as basis to powerfully develop other patriotic forces.

In the specific condition of the South Vietnam society, the democratic problem plays a particularly important role, because with its false agrarian reform policy, the U.S. imperialists-sponsored puppet administration has done its utmost to grab the land allotted to the peasants during the war of resistance against the French ; what this administration called agrarian reform was actually the distribution of a small acreage of land to its faithful lackeys. It is precisely for this reason that the South Vietnam Liberation National Front has raised the slogan *"to carry out land rent reduction and then to solve the land problem for the peasants so that the tillers will have land to till"*. During the last ten years, the peasants in the South have received in distribution more than 1.5 million hectares of land, or nearly three times over the acreage of land allotted during the former resistance war. Most of these lands belonged to the imperialists and reactionary big landdlords who had followed the enemy. This distribution of land to the peasants bear a paramount significance because the people's war is a revolutionary war waged by the masses of which the peasants make up over 90 per cent. As the peasants in the South have by tradition an indomitable fighting spirit, the fact that they have received now vital interest from the revolution is for them a stimulus and they can organize themselves into a mighty force to wage a long resistance war.

In South Vietnam, not only has the puppet administration grabbed the land of the peasants, but it has daily violated the lives and property of the people, sprayed toxic chemicals to destroy the crops, coerced the inhabitants into leaving their homes and villages to be herded into strategic hamlets. In the town, the economic policy which depends on the U.S. imperialists has caused the bankruptcy of the native manufacturers and traders and a serious unemployment among the toiling people. That is why the democratic slogan has also another content which is *to improve the people's livelihood* and to demand *the implementation of an independent economic policy.*

Democracy has furthermore a political content of paramount importance which is to demand the carrying out of democratic liberties in opposition to the fascist dictatorial regime. The U.S. imperialists usually boast that the administrations under their sway have pursued a policy of "freedom", that they have also written down "democratic liberties" in their constitutions. However, in practice, from the very beginning these administrations have become fascist dictatorial powers. That is why the slogans *"to institute a broad and progressive democratic regime"*, to guarantee democratic liberties demanding the implementation of article 14-C of the Geneva Agreement, to oppose discriminations against former resistance members, etc... have responded to the urgent requirements of all strata of the population and have effectively urged the broad masses of people to rise against the enemy.

At present our country is temporarily partitioned into two zones having each a different social regime. The revolutionary task ahead of the South Vietnam people is to overthrow the U.S. imperialists and their henchmen and to win independence and democracy. Not only have the great majority of grass-root masses realized the necessity of carrying out this task but they have aspired to take the revolution to a new height. Meanwhile the national bourgeoisie and a section of the middle classes, in the one hand, oppose U.S.-imperialism out of nationalism, and on the other, want to defend the interests of their own classes. In order to rally the largest majority of people, the Front has laid down appropriate home and foreign policies; internally it advocates the *promotion of national industry and trade and development of the national economy;* externally it advocates a diplomatic policy of *peace and neutrality.* The slogan "neutrality" has a great echo among the upper classes in South Vietnam and a widespread repercussion among the officers, soldiers and civil servants of the enemy's administration; it has received the greatest approval and support from abroad. Is it necessary to stress the *requirement for peace* and the *step taken to reunify the country,* because genuine peace is the aspiration of every one in the South, the more so since it has experienced twenty years of continual warfare; because reunification is the profound aspiration of every Vietnamese; Vietnam has ever been one and indivisible.

Because the goal of its struggle is just and conforms to the fundamental aspirations of the people, and is mentioned in its platform, it can be said that at present *the South Vietnam Liberation National Front is able to rally the overwhelming majority of fourteen million people of the South, to mobilize, organize and lead our compatriots there in the war for national liberation and salvation.* It is obvious that this war which bears a national character as well as a class character, is mainly a war for national salvation against the U.S. aggressive imperialists and their myrmidons. This is *a people's war in a new historic condition* in South Vietnam.

*
* *

The liberation war waged by the South Vietnam people is *an all-out war.*

In this "special war" the enemy fights us mainly by military means but he also lays stress on political activities, the "cong dan vu activities" in order to win over the people and eagerly to penetrate into South Vietnam through economic and cultural media, etc. The liberation war waged by our people over there covers many fields : military, political, economic and cultural.

a) Our people cherish peace by tradition. In the early days of the successful August Revolution, when the Democratic Republic of Vietnam has just been set up, we have done our best to win peace by signing the preliminary Agreement with the French government. But historical facts have shown that while we

51

loved peace, the imperialists and colonialists did their utmost to kindle war. In the end, to defend the vital interests of our country, all our people have risen up, used armed violence and revolutionary struggle against counter-revolutionary violence, against the aggressive war of the French colonialists propped up by the U.S. imperialists. And we have carried the day.

In 1954, after the signing of the Geneva Agreement, from North to South, all our people longed for peace ; they made every effort to maintain and consolidate it and fought against all acts sabotaging the Geneva Agreement in the South ; while the U.S. imperialists and the puppet administration used counter-revolutionary violence to terrorize and massacre them, our people have put up during many years, a most valiant political struggle against the enemy. In fact, this struggle has testified once again that *to the counter-revolutionary violence of the enemy, our people must definitely oppose revolutionary violence.*

At the price of their hard-won experiences, our compatriots in the South realized that the fundamental trend of imperialism and its lackeys is violence and war, that is why *the most correct path to be followed by the peoples to liberate themselves is revolutionary violence and revolutionary war.* This path conforms strictly to the ethics and the fundamentals of Marxism-Leninism on class struggle, on the state and the revolution. Only by revolutionary violence can the masses defeat aggressive imperialism and its lackeys and overthrow the reactionary administration to take power. When the U.S. imperialists stepped up armed intervention in the South, the revolutionary struggle waged by our people turned into a widespread people's war, which has won greater and greater successes with every passing day.

The experiences gained in the revolutionary struggle put up by all our people during the last decades and by our southern compatriots over the past ten years have proved that revolutionary violence and revolutionary war is the correct path followed by the peoples who want to rise up and smash the domination of the colonialist imperialists and their lackeys ; in definite conditions they are the real possibilities for these peoples to liberate themselves.

b) Revolutionary violence takes up many forms : political violence, armed violence, and armed violence combined with political violence. Basing ourselves on our absolute superiority in the political field, and on the policy of the enemy who uses military as well as political means to quell the revolution, our southern compatriots are now using political violence combined with armed violence against the enemy. They have known how to take advantage of and to develop the valuable experiences gained by all our people in the revolutionary struggles they have waged up to the present time. These various forms of violence have led our people to brilliant victories. We have also known how to creatively apply the experiences gained in the recent revolutionary struggles in the world such as in Cuba and Algeria, where great successes have been achieved as the result of a skilful co-ordination between armed struggle and political struggle.

It can be said that one of the striking particularities of the revolutionary war in the South, of the comprehensive character of this war, is that it *is developing simultaneously in two forms — political struggle and armed struggle — in a long period.*

Political struggle plays a very fundamental role because our basic strength and the enemy's basic weakness lie in the political field, because the enemy schemes to deceive the people by political means, because the South Vietnam people are by tradition indomitable in political struggle and have a very high political and organizational spirit. Once the people have a high revolutionary spirit, they are always a huge force, play a decisive role and are a deciding factor of the revolutionary struggle. However, particularly in the present era, the toiling worker-peasant masses and progressive people of the world have made big strides on the road of revolutionary struggle; particularly in the South our people have been tempered for decades in political and armed struggles; while the administration and army serving the U.S. imperialists are very weak in the political field, our people have ample possibilities to develop extensively their political strength and to exploit the great shortcomings of the enemy in order to secure victory for us.

Armed struggle is a high form of revolutionary struggle; it *is playing a very fundamental and* important role. Only with the support of armed struggle, can the masses bring into play their political authority. As the enemy is using counter-revolutionary war against the people, to overthrow his domination, it is absolutely necessary for the people to annihilate and disintegrate the puppet army In the specific condition of South Vietnam, armed struggle should closely combine with political struggle; at the same time it should abide by the laws on warfare and plays its role of annihilating as many enemy's forces as possible.

c) In the South, from the two major currents of struggle mentioned above, the masses have formed and built up a very mighty political force and an ever powerful revolutionary armed force.

The *political army of the masses* includes all ages and sexes and established bases everywhere — in the lowlands and highlands, in town and country. This army has risen up and smashed to pieces the enemy's rural administration, destroyed a great number of strategic hamlets, carried out agitation work among the puppet soldiers and urged tens of thousands of them to go over to the side of the people; it has fought against conscription and corvée, against the spraying of toxic chemicals, repression of religions, arson and eviction of houses ; it has demanded the protection of human lives and property, the improvement of the people's livelihood, the application of democracy, the punishment of Ngo Dinh Diem's henchmen and the expulsion of the U.S. imperialists from South Vietnam. This political army has now used a legal form for its struggle, turned what is illegal into legal ; it is never threatened by terror and bloodshed ; it has advanced bare-handed and used a patriotic language to convince the enemy troops. Nobody can forget the scene in which tens of thousands of peasants have broken through the cordon of bayonets, rushed into town and stirred the streets with shouts of hatred and indignation. Nobody can forget the picture of a mountain girl who threw herself in front of an enemy bulldozer which was destroying her village to build a strategic road; the image of a South Vietnamese girl who, with her body, prevented an enemy cannon from shelling her village.

While workers, pupils and students have played a worthwhile role in the political struggle in the towns, the women peasants were constantly on the front rank of the struggle in the countryside. When this political army temporarily stops direct struggle, it will engage in the production of foods and weapons, do afforestation work, dig trenches, make spikes, fence their fighting villages or perform their duty as transporters, scouts, messengers to help the armymen.

At first, *the revolutionary armed forces* of South Vietnam were the self-defence units and armed propaganda units which saw the light of day in the fire of the movement of political struggles of the people. Then bigger units appeared with the extensive development of the militia and guerilla and with guerilla warfare. At present the armed forces of the South Vietnam people have grown very swiftly in strength under three forms which co-ordinate closely with one another in military operations: *the militia and guerilla, the local troops and the regular army.* Though still young and fighting in very hard and difficult conditions, the *South Vietnam Liberation army* has successively defeated the enemy and has now raised the degree of its political consciousness, and increased its equipment, mobility and fighting strength. In equipment, it mainly relies on the arms and ammunition taken from the enemy and increases its strength in the course of fighting; it is closely linked with the population. Like the Vietnam People's army, the brother South Vietnam Liberation army is not only an army which fights heroically but an army which is remarkable in production and excellent in every work; it can annihilate great numbers of enemy troops at the front and actively make propaganda among the population; it can successfully carry out agitation work among enemy troops, and work painstakingly to fend for itself where supply from outside meets with difficulties.

In face of a modernly equipped enemy who has a great mobility and all means for its intelligence service, but a very low morale, the South Vietnam Liberation army has known how to analyse the strong and weak points of the enemy; it has fought unremittingly and got the upper hand of the enemy; together with the inhabitants, it has destroyed strategic hamlets, victoriously resisted small raids and large-scale raids as well, it has laid ambushes, carried out sudden attacks and annihilated whole companies, even whole regiments, stormed small posts, then bigger posts and even a whole sub-sector. The Liberation troops have attacked communication lines (roads and waterways) of the enemy, burned petrol depots and ammunition dumps, attacked airfields, sunk warships and killed American advisers in the very centre of Saigon. In the recent past, the armed struggle of our people in the South has developed into *a quite extensive guerilla war of a fairly high level.* It can be said that at present, guerilla warfare in the South develops at a quicker tempo than during the resistance against the French and faces more difficult fighting conditions. The Liberation troops have performed a great number of heroic deeds. During the arduous and fierce struggle it has waged, there appeared *many examples of immortal sacrifice and great heroism,* which continue the glorious tradition of the nation, the revolution and the former resistance war — Tru Van Tho plugged a loophole with his body; Mai Van The cut himself one of his arms to continue the fighting; Nguyen Viet Khai had three helicopters shot down to his credit; Ly Van So damaged three amphibious cars; a group at Ap Bac got its fame; the Long Trung guerillas persistently resisted a 29-day raid, etc.

The Liberation army is now heroically annihilating the U.S.-sponsored puppet army commanded by American advisers. It made its appearance only a few years ago, yet it is the terror of the enemy who has gradually realized that, it is not he who in future will annihilate us but it is the Liberation army which will defeat him. The heroic South Vietnam Liberation army deserves the confidence of our southern compatriots and of the fatherland.

d) After the victories of the political struggle and armed struggle, the liberated areas have been broadened, running from the High Plateaux of Central Vietnam to the Mekong delta. The building of these areas in the political, economic and cultural fields has become an important task and is all the more important for the liberation war in the South. At present the liberated areas are separated from one another but entangle with the enemy-controlled areas, or reach out-of-the-way places; they cover the provinces of the densely peopled delta and even draw near big and small towns. The liberated areas are not only firm guerilla bases, but are also built to become shining models of a new life, of a new regime in opposition to the gloomy state and stifling atmosphere of the enemy-controlled areas.

Under the direction of the Front, the people of the liberated areas are obviously masters of the land and are doing their best to manage and build their life along progressive lines. Democratic liberties, freedom of belief, freedom of business, equality among nationalities are respected and widely implemented. Cultural, social, educational activities and the health service are progressing. A healthy patriotic art and literature of a mass character contributes to the mobilization of the people for the struggle.

Here, our compatriots are freed from the plunder and exploitation by the enemy; they are enthusiastically tackling production, improving their method of work, raising their livelihood and at the same time actively pooling their efforts to wage the war of resistance. Here, the economic, agrarian and religious policies of the Front, and the policy dealing with the bourgeois and foreign residents, the policy regarding the puppet soldiers and officers who go over to the side of the people are clearly defined and readjusted.

At present the liberated areas have played their strategic role in the liberation war and have brought great influence to bear on the inhabitants of the enemy-controlled areas including the towns. The liberated areas are precisely the first pictures of free and independent South Vietnam in future; they will certainly be expanded and consolidated and will become the regions in which the future regime of the South will be applied after the victory of the liberation war.

*

* *

The liberation war of our people in the South is *long, arduous, self-supporting but it will certainly be victorious.*

It will certainly be long and arduous because at the beginning our forces were politically very powerful but materially weak, while the forces of the enemy were very weak in the political field but by far more powerful than ours in the material point of view. Time, persevering and strenuous efforts, overcoming great difficulties and a correct trend of struggle are factors which can gradually bring about a change in the relation of forces — from weak to strong for us and from strong to weak for the enemy. We must be fully prepared in ideology and organization to carry out a long resistance war in most difficult and hard conditions because the enemy of our nation and people — the U.S. imperialists and their henchmen — is a very cruel and die-hard enemy, because to him, South Vietnam occupies quite an important strategic position; surely he is not to give up easily unless obliged to do so by the ever increasing strength of our people.

Formerly, in our war against the French coloniaiists and U.S. interventionists, we put forth the slogan to carry out a long term resistance. At present, in the war for liberation waged by our people in the South, we must also grasp this slogan to win victory. We must realize that in this war, conditions differ in every respect : our people have been tempered ; they have many experiences and a great courage ; the enemy has enormous weaknesses in the political field ; the international situation develops in our favour ; the guiding line of the Front is very correct and creative and is able to combine the experiences of revolutionary struggle of our people with those of the brother countries ; that is why, while grasping the principle of putting up a long-term resistance war, our people in the South must also fully realize the new favourable conditions in order to march forward steadily, energetically and with confidence, and to do our best to take advantage of the weaknesses of the enemy and to create new propitious conditions for us.

The secret to overcome our difficulties and improve our successes and to make time constantly work for our people and the revolution, is actively and rapidly to build, maintain, foster and gather our strength in every respect so that our force grows stronger in the fight while that of the enemy grows weaker and weaker.

The liberation war of our southern compatriots must be mainly *self-supporting* although international assistance is important and invaluable, because it is a revolutionary struggle waged by a people who, not content to be enslaved, rise up to liberate themselves ; because, however advantageous they may be, the objective conditions from without are efficacious only when they are facilitated by the efforts from within ; because, though the North is a firmer and firmer base of the revolutionary struggle for the whole country, yet the policy of the government of the Democratic Republic of Vietnam is constantly to respect the stipulations of the Geneva Agreements and resolutely to struggle for the peaceful reunification of the country, thereby winning further support and sympathy from the world for the revolutionary struggle in the South. For this reason the South Vietnam people must do their best to stand on their own feet in order to win victory.

In the former resistance war against the French colonialists and the U.S. interventionists our southern compatriots set a bright example of self-supply and self-procurement, having only rudimentary weapons and bamboo spears to fight the aggressors. At present, in their war for liberation against the U.S. imperialists and their lackeys, our compatriots have once again started from scratch : from having no power and no army, as yet they resolutely rose against a cruel enemy. The reality of the last ten years in the South has thoroughly substantiated the correctness of the slogan of self-supply and self-procurement and confirmed the possibility of the heroic people of South Vietnam to wage direct revolution and struggle for self-liberation.

The war for liberation of our southern people is long and arduous but *it will certainly win final victory.*

In the former great war of resistance, all our people, including our southern compatriots, have defeated the old colonialism of the French imperialists propped up by the U.S. interventionists. In the present war for national salvation, we are pitted against a new enemy — U.S. imperialism and its henchmen — who is using a new kind of war to conquer our country. The problem is : who will win in the South ? Have our southern compatriots every possibility to defeat the U.S. imperialists and their lackeys in their aggressive war of a special type ?

It needs not wait until the South Vietnam people win final victory, but right now, with the great victories of strategic importance won by the revolution in the South, we can assess *that the South Vietnam people will win and the U.S. imperialists and their lackeys will be shamefully defeated.*

The U.S. imperialists and their stooges have called *"special"* the war they have unleashed, ; what has it as special ? Unlike French imperialism formerly, U.S. imperialism applies neo-colonialism in the South ! As in the political and economic field, neo-colonialism robs and oppresses the peoples of various countries through puppet administrations, when it is necessary to wage a war of aggression, the new-colonialists deem it better to use the reactionary troops of the quisling as main forces, while the U.S. imperialists play the role of directing the war and supplying money and weapons, with Americain troops taking part in the war to a certain extent, the fewer the better. What is dangerous in the special war is that it hides the aggressive face of the U.S. imperialists, thereby it can split the rank of our people, and affect the unity and combativeness of our nation. The weakness of the special war is that in nature it is a war of aggression all the same and its future depends a great deal on the strength of the reactionary forces and on the puppet administration and army.

Abiding by this definition, immediately after the restoration of peace, the U.S. imperialists have waged a real special war in South Vienam. The unilateral war unleashed by the Ngo Dinh Diem administration for many years to shatter the rank of the people was precisely the special war conducted by the U.S imperialists with the blood of the Vietnamese people, with U.S. dollars and weapons under the direction of Washington and the direct command of American military personnel still in small number at that time. In some respect, that special war was waged when conditions were still relatively favourable to the U.S. imperialists' neo-colonialism. However, the South Vietnam people have realized from the very beginning the aggressive nature of colonialism — old or new — and have therefore waged a fierce political struggle against the enemy. This struggle has obtained great successes, especially at the end of 1959 and in 1960, and has seriously endangered the U.S.-sponsored puppet administration. We may consider this *grave danger for the Ngo Dinh Diem regime as the first defeat of strategic character of the U.S. imperialists' new-type aggressive war.*

When the U.S. imperialists overtly stepped up armed intervention, mapped out the Staley-Taylor plan, and officially made mention of the so-called "special war", on the one hand, U.S. aids pouring in South Vietnam were greater, weapons introduced there were in larger quantities, and American advisers and soldiers were more numerous, thereby materially increasing the puppet military forces, but on the other hand the aggressive face of neo-colonialism was exposed and the indignation of our southern compatriots and their determination in struggle were growing. The political situation becomes all the more unfavourable to the enemy and favourable to us. This is precisely one of the principal factors which contribute to the most rapid and powerful development of the people's war in South Vietnam and to the failure of the Staley-Taylor plan. *This failure is also the second great strategic setback of the new-type aggressive war of the U.S. imperialists' neo-colonialism.*

At present the U.S. imperialists are stepping up armed intervention in the South, affording greater assistance in every respect and increasing again the number of U.S. military advisers and combat units. This is quite a great war effort of the U.S. imperialists which can create new difficulties to our people in the South. But on the other hand, the special character of this aggressive war loses more and more its effectiveness owing to the outright intervention of the U.S. imperialists. For this reason, the front uniting all our people against the U.S. imperialists has broadened day by day and the rank of the quislings splits further. As has been said above, in practice, the struggle of the past six months has not yet brought any further results to the U.S. imperialists and their stooges but only caused them greater and greater setbacks and losses.

While discussing the special war, the American generals usually emphasize the *military economic, political and psychological* side of the war. The U.S.

ruling circles have many a time come to the conclusion that the failure of the Diem-Nhu brothers was due to the fact that they could not win the people over to their side. The U.S. imperialists have explained to the quislings the necessity to win the people's heart. But can the puppets win the people's confidence with their policy of repression and terror, treachery and deceit regarding freedom. and sham independence? As in nature, they run counter to the people's interests, they cannot win the people to their side. The southern people resist them with might and main. That is why the political means used in the special war and psychological war against the South Vietnam people will certainly meet with failure.

The special war needs quite a powerful puppet army having great effectives, a full equipment and a high degree of mobility. At present the military effort of the U.S. imperialists is aimed at building up such a reactionary army. But in the end, owing to the unjust political goal of the war, most of the Vietnamese who serve in the puppet army, are not willing to fight and kill their compatriots and their fighting spirit was sinking.

Recently, in the special war the establishment of the *system of strategic hamlets* has been considered as the newest and most efficient experiment conducted in a counter-revolutionary war against the people. The U.S. imperialists and their myrmidons have gathered their human and material resources to set up these hamlets in order to re-impose their yoke on the inhabitants, to break all relations between the population and the liberation army. However, when millions of peasants rise up together, no policy on prosperity zones, no "state policy" on strategic hamlets can overcome their stubborn combativeness. In the South, the powerful solidarity in struggle of millions of peasant masses has rendered inefficacious the huge system of high walls and deep moats of strategic hamlets, destroyed thousands of these strongly-built hamlets immediately after their building, and turned thousands of others into fighting villages to resist the enemy. The disintegration of the strategic hamlet "state policy" at present is a most bitter failure of the special war. Of late, the U.S imperialists and their stooges have changed the name of strategic hamlets into *new-life hamlets,* but certainly this will not in the least raise the efficiency of these hamlets.

What perfidious scheme will the U.S. imperialists have in store in future? They are plotting to dispatch more American troops to South Vietnam, intensify the special war and turn it into a local war, then their neo-colonialism will be exposed. However, with the repeated victories won by our southern compatriots in the war for liberation, in the present international conjuncture, before doing so, the U.S. ruling circles, including the topmost war-mongers in the Pentagon, will surely have to weigh the pros and cons before embarking on such a dangerous war adventure Certainly they have not forgotten that with half a million troops of their expeditionary corps, the French imperialists were routed in Indo-China, with eight hundred thousand soldiers, they were defeated in Algeria and with over a million soldiers, the U.S. imperialists and their lackeys were beaten in Korea

If at present the imperialists dare kindle a local war, certainly, they will meet with a bitterer and more shameful failure.

Who will win in the South ? Certainly the South Vietnam people will win and the U.S. imperialists will be defeated.

After 10 years of fierce and hard struggle, our compatriots in the South have won victories of strategic importance. The liberated area has been expanded, the people's force has been increased and the revolutionary armed forces have grown rapidly and powerfully.

Our southern compatriots have a lofty, a *just* goal The U.S. imperialists and their henchmen have all the sinews of war — money and weapons — but they are the invaders and traitors to our country, they only lack the national and democratic banner. That is why our people will certainly win and the U.S. imperialists and their lackeys will be defeated

Millions united as one man, our people are gathering in a broad rank within the South Vietnam Liberation National Front, while the U.S. imperialists and their lackeys are hated by our people ; their social bases shrink and their inner contradictions deepen. This is the reason why our people will win and the U.S. imperialists and their stooges will be defeated.

In the South our people have a new-type revolutionary army, a people's army — the heroic South Vietnam Liberation army — which, despite its inferiority in number compared with the enemy. is a steel tempered army , it has a very high fighting spirit, is born from the people, fights for the Fatherland and the people and enjoys an unstinted support and care from the entire people ; on the side of the enemy, the puppet army, though in greater number, has a lower and lower fighting spirit ; among its rank opposition to war has appeared and is likely to spread. For this reason, our people will win and the U S. imperialists and their henchmen will be defeated.

The war for liberation waged at present by our compatriots in the South is enjoying an immense support and sympathy from all progressive mankind. Conversely, the aggressive war unleashed by the U.S imperialists are condemned all over the world. This explains why our people will win and the U.S imperialists and their lackeys will be defeated.

Furthermore, we know that, in a war, the political, military, economic, and geographical conditions and international assistance on both sides give only the chance of victory or defeat but cannot bring victory or defeat to one side. Victory or defeat depends on the own efforts and the self-conscious ability of man, especially in the direction of the war In this connection we are elated to know that the *political and military line of the South Vietnam Liberation National Front is very precise* and is the source of great victories of our people in the South.

At present South Vietnam stands on *the front-line* of the struggle against imperialism headed by U.S. imperialism.

South Vietnam is the *vanguard fighter* of the national liberation movement in the present era

At the same time it is considered as one of the *most active parts of progressive mankind* now struggling stubbornly against the warlike policy and for world peace.

In South Vietnam, once again the hard-boiled truth of our era has substantiated that : *in the present world conditions, when a nation — however weak and small it may be — rises up according to a correct political line, and struggles stubbornly for independence and peace, it has ample possibility to triumph over the powerful army of the aggressive imperialists and the treacherous clique, to thwart all aggressive plots of the imperialists and old or new colonialists*

The international significance of the war for liberation of our southern compatriots lies in that *this war has set an example of stubborn but victorious struggle of a weak and small nation against U.S. imperialism, contributes* to corroborate the fundamentals of Marxism-Leninism on the national democratic revolution of colonial, semi-colonial, semi-colonial and semi-feudal countries, and avert the harmful influence of modern revisionism in the national-liberation movement.

The great significance of the war for liberation waged by our southern compatriots is that : *the revolutionary war of the people can triumph over the special war of the U.S. imperialists.* And the failure of the special war unleashed by the U.S. imperialists in South Vietnam would mean that this war can be defeated anywhere in the world

The most heroic war for liberation waged by our southern compatriots demonstrates that in our era, the new invention is not only nuclear weapons but the new and very great creation of the masses is the people's war (developed to a high degree) against the war of aggression of imperialism — be it in the form of old colonialism or new colonialism. *People's war is always victorious and invincible.*

IV

Before the danger of a heavier failure, the U.S. ruling circles are striving to retrieve their present situation in South Vietnam.

The U.S. political circles and influential personalities have brought forward many opinions, and devised varied military measures not excluding the political ones. This clearly reflected the American embarrassment and deadlock after ten years of intervention and aggression in the south of our country.

After the signing of the Geneva Agreements with the fame and force that the U.S.A. had at that time, all American political and military figures were optimistic, thinking that South Vietnam was an easy prey. At the birth of the Staley-Taylor plan though being no more optimistic as five, six years before, a great many people among the U.S aggressive circles were still confident in the special war as a means to pacify South Vietnam within 18 months. But now, after ten years of successive failures, especially the bitter ones over the past three years, their optimism and confidence have vanished ; they begin to squabble with one another — and the squabble is growing hotter — about the cause of their defeat, and the measures to restore the situation. During the discussion, they come to agree on one point : their hope of winning swiftly in South Vietnam is lost, but they are still at variance on the way how to get out of the present tunnel with no end in view

Due to its extreme warlike and reactionary nature the Johnson government is striving to continue the war, and clinging to its aggressive colonial policy in the South. This is easy to understand, if we examine the strategic position of South Vietnam with regard to the whole of the American warlike scheme in Indo-China and South-East Asia, and the important significance of the first experiment of their special warfare in the South aimed at repressing the movement for independence of various peoples, Johnson has many a time said about the determination of the U.S.A. to stay in South Vietnam at all costs. Therefore, it is quite certain that the U S. government will certainly *continue to intensify the special war* it has kindled, and further speed up every military activity, with a view to boosting the morale and bridging the gap between its lackeys who are wavering and being at variance with one another, and endeavouring to win some victory before finding another solution.

Simultaneously with the pushing forward of the aggressive war in South Vietnam, the U.S. imperialists will further *intensify the provocation and sabotage in North Vietnam,* hoping to create more difficulties to our entire people's struggle for national reunification. The fact that the Americans are obliged to increase these acts at present, at this time when they are deeply bogged down in the South, shows that they are in a bitter passive situation. It is precisely because they are defeated by the southern people that they must take such adventurous measures. It is certain that in intensifying these acts the U.S. imperialists can threaten no one but bring upon themselves further shameful failures and hatred of the entire people from North to South. How can these acts prevent the northern people from giving their unshakable support to their southern compatriots' patriotic struggle. How can they lessen the latter's iron-like confidence in and sincere sympathy with the socialist North, the revolutionary base of the whole country.

Due to their acute crisis in South Vietnam, the U.S. imperialists have schemed to intensify their armed intervention in the Kingdom of Laos and threaten the neutrality of the Kingdom of Cambodia, with a view to creating tension in Indo-China and South-East Asia. They want to rely upon these provocative acts and this display of force to screen their defeats in South Vietnam, and mislead the world opinion which is severely condemning their aggressive war in the South.

To serve these dark warlike schemes, thousands of U.S. military personnel, U.S. weapons, ammunition and war means have been recently introduced into South Vietnam. At the same time the U.S.A. has carried on the transfer of its army and warships to South-East Asia.

In face of the U.S. policy of adding fuel on fire, and intensifying the sabotage of peace in Indo-China and

South-East Asia our people in North Vietnam set themselves extremely heavy responsibilities and tasks : *to strengthen the defence of socialist North Vietnam, to protect our people's peaceful and creative labour : to' be determined to support our southern people's patriotic struggle, to push forward the struggle for peaceful reunification of the Fatherland ; to strengthen the solidarity with and the support to the Laotian and Cambodian peoples in the defence of their independence, sovereignty and territorial integrity, and in their struggle against the U.S. intervention and aggression.* This responsibility is very heavy, and this task very high, however with our thorough revolutionary spirit, profound patriotism, and just international spirit, we will certainly discharge our responsibility before the nation and the world's people.

The Resolution of the Third Party National Congress has stressed : "Vietnam is one, the Vietnamese people is one, our entire people's will for national reunification is unshakable, the final victory will certainly be ours". In the light of the Resolution, we have clearly realized that North Vietnam is building socialism, South Vietnam is carrying on the liberation war, these two tasks have a close relation with each other, and help each other. While carrying on the second sacred resistance war to liberate themselves our southern compatriots also aim at checking and smashing the U.S. imperialists' scheme of aggression against our whole country. Inversely, to peacefully build socialism in North Vietnam, and to strengthen the force of the North in every respect : political, economic and national defence, is precisely the most decisive task with regard to the development of the whole Vietnamese revolution, and the struggle for national reunification. Over the past ten years, this ideological trend has unceasingly mobilized 16 million northern people eagerly to work and record brilliant achievements in the building up of their country, without halting before any sacrifice 14 million southern people are heroically fighting to win back and firmly defend every inch of land of Vietnam. *North and South Vietnam are under the same roof, the South is the front-line, the North is the political and moral support of the Fatherland.* North Vietnam has the task of building socialism and making it a firm basis for the southern people's patriotic struggle, and the struggle for national reunification. Today in the North the *movement for sworn brotherhood between the northern and southern people,* a lively expression of the North and South Vietnam kinship, has gained town and country, the *successive emulation drives for our southern kith-and-kin and national reunification,* have brought in the highest labour productivity. "Everyone redoubles his efforts to show his gratitude to his southern kith-and-kin", this warm appeal of President Ho Chi Minh, the beloved leader of the entire people, is urging every one of us to work.

Facing the U.S. imperialists' and their lackeys' scheme of intensifying provocative and sabotage acts in the North our people in North Vietnam must *strive to strengthen and consolidate national defence, defend security, and further raise their revolutionary vigilance and their hatred for the enemy* We must clearly realize that to build the North and defend it are twin tasks. Each of us in North Vietnam must be aware that the economic building and development of production is the central task, at the same time he must always pay attention to combining economic building with strengthening of national defence, strive to raise the defence work in all respects, be ready to cope with all provocations and sabotages of the enemy, and smash every of his adventurous acts. All the commandos of the U.S. imperialists' lackeys in South Vietnam as well as those of Chiang Kai-shek commanded by the U.S. recently introduced secretly into North Vietnam, were surrounded and completely annihilated by our armymen and people. This shows the high vigilance and sharp readiness for fighting of North Vietnam's armymen and people. We must develop this good point to continue dealing heavier blows at the U.S. imperialists and their flunkeys if they pursue their aggression against socialist North Vietnam.

The armed forces — the people's army, the people's armed security forces, the people's militia and the self-defence units — must clearly realize their heavy responsibility in the present situation of the country : North Vietnam is building in peace. South Vietnam is carrying on the liberation war ; over the past ten years, though being heavily defeated by the southern people, the U.S. imperialists do not want to draw useful lessons and are pursuing the aggressive war on half of our country. Before the complete victory of our people the extremely hard and complex struggle between our people and the U.S imperialists still goes on. Therefore we must *further raise the tradition of determination to fight and to win, be always vigilant and ready for fighting, heighten the spirit to implement the orders, be united and closely act in unison, boldly wipe out the enemy, and be determined successfully to fulfil every military task entrusted by the Party and Government.* We must further develop the spirit of readiness for fighting of a revolutionary army, firmly hold every weapon, and instruments of war, and defend the territorial integrity, air space and territorial waters of the Democratic Republic of Vietnam. We are certain to defeat every wicked scheme of the U.S. imperialists.

Recently, simultaneously with the intensifying of provocative and sabotage acts in North Vietnam, the strafing and shelling of the Laotian people's liberated zone, the violation of the Cambodian border, the bellicose Americans have still clamoured that they will strafe and shell the territory of the Democratic Republic of Vietnam, and extend the war to the North. We warn the U.S. imperialists, "Should the U.S. bellicists be rash enough to attack the North, the entire people of the country would stand up as one man to smash to smithereens their aggression and completely defeat them all over the country" To attack the North is to attack a socialist country; it is certain that the peoples of the brother socialist countries, of South-East Asia, and the progressive people the world over will wholeheartedly support us.

The July 15, 1964 Statement of our Government has said that there is only one issue for the U.S. imperialists in South Vietnam:

1. The U.S. Government must respect the sovereignty, independence, unity, and territorial integrity of Vietnam, refrain from interfering in her internal affairs.

2. The U.S. Government must put an end to its aggressive war in South Vietnam, withdraw all its troops and weapons from there and leave the South Vietnamese people to settle their own internal affairs by themselves in accordance with the programme of the South Vietnam National Liberation Front.

3. The peaceful reunification of Vietnam is an internal affair of the Vietnamese people, it will be solved in accordance with the spirit of the political programme of the Vietnam Fatherland Front and the programme of the South Vietnam Liberation National Front.

Except for this there is no other way out. If the U.S. imperialists continue their war of aggression against South Vietnam, they will be certainly defeated by the southern people and will be finally doomed to a complete failure. If they rashly extend the war to the North, this would be a suicide for them.

The successes recorded during ten years of peaceful construction in North Vietnam are filling each of us with enthusiasm *The socialist building in Vietnam will certainly succeed.*

The successes of the revolution in South Vietnam during the past ten years are powerfully mobilizing every one of us. *The revolutionary work to liberate South Vietnam, and peacefully reunify the Fatherland will certainly succeed brilliantly.*

Today no reactionary force in the world can prevent 30 million people of our whole country from carrying out their sacred aspiration, that is *to build a peaceful, unified, independent, democratic, prosperous and powerful Vietnam.*

July, 1964

ANNEX

PRINCIPAL EVENTS IN SOUTH VIETNAM
DURING THE PAST TEN YEARS (1954-1964) *

1954

July 7, 1954 Two months after the victory of the Vietnam People's Army at Dien Bien Phu (May 7, 1954), under American pressure, the French have to let down Buu Loc and recognize Ngo Dinh Diem — a Catholic mandarin trained and fostered by the United States at Lakewood (New Jersey) since 1951 — as Prime Minister of the Bao Dai administration

July 21, 1954 The Geneva Agreements on Indo-China are signed Though the U.S government's delegate, Bedell Smith, has stated that "the United States will refrain from the threat or the use of force to disturb the Agreements", U.S. President Eisenhower declares "The United States has not itself been party to, or bound by, the decisions taken by the Conference"

August 1, 1954 The Saigon - Cholon peace movement starts its activities with the following aim to consolidate peace in Indo-China, ensure democratic freedoms and achieve Vietnam's reunification through nation-wide free general elections. Lawyer Nguyen Huu Tho is one of its promoters. From Saigon-Cholon

---

Collected by the Foreign Languages Publishing House

the movement spreads to all the provinces in South Vietnam and involves broad masses of the people including high-ranking officials of the Diem administration.

September 8, 1954. Setting up of the South-East Asia Treaty Organization in Manila (Philippines) grouping the United States, Great Britain, France, Australia, Thailand, the Philippines and Pakistan This bloc puts South Vietnam, Laos and Cambodia under its "protection"

November 20, 1954. In Washington, J.F Dulles, U S Secretary of State, officially informs French Premier Mendès-France that beginning 1955 the United States would send its aid directly to the Diem administration and not through the French as formerly

*   *

Right after the armistice (July 20, 1954) the U S -Diem brazenfacedly terrorized the South Vietnam people, made reprisals against and persecuted former Resistance members under the so-called "movement of indictment of Communists" which the U.S.-sponsored South Vietnam administration raised to the level of a "state policy" On the other hand, in November 1954, the U.S.-Diem repressed the peace movement and arrested many of its promoters among them Lawyer Nguyen Huu Tho The South Vietnam people energetically reacted by pushing ahead the movement against "indictment of Communists"

1955

February 4, 1955. The Government of the D.R V proposes to the South Vietnam administration that normal relations between South and North Vietnam be re-established to create favourable conditions for a consultative conference about national reunification elections.

February 12, 1955. Ngo Dinh Diem makes known that U.S Gen. O'Daniel would take over the training of the South Vietnam Army from the Command of the French Union forces

April 26, 1955. With American help, Ngo Dinh Diem launches his army against the pro-French armed forces of the Binh Xuyen clique and the religious sects, causing bloodshed and fire right in Saigon-Cholon This clash causes 7,000 dead, 14,000 wounded and destroyed over 20,000 houses Let down by the French, the religious sects and the Binh Xuyen clique could not resist Diem.

June 6, 1955 and July 19, 1955. The Government of the D.R.V twice sends notes to the South Vietnam administration proposing that a consultative conference be convened on July 20, 1955 as laid down in the 1954 Geneva Agreement.

July 3, 1955. Big meeting of the Saigon-Cholon people demanding the release of the arrested members of the Relief Committee (set up after the bloody clashes between the Diem troops and the forces of the Binh Xuyen clique and the religious sects) and the convening of a consultative conference about general elections

July 16, 1955 and August 9, 1955. The Ngo Dinh Diem administration declares it opposes the implementation of the Geneva Agreement and rejects the consultative conference about general elections under the pretext that the southern administration "could not be bound by this Agreement".

July 20, 1955 Diem has his agents organize a meeting in Saigon in protest of the Geneva Agreement and sack the premises of the International Commission

October 23, 1955 Diem organizes a fraudulous "referendum" at gun-point to "dethrone Bao Dai" and appoint himself "head of State".

October 26, 1955 : Diem proclaims the establishment of the "Republic of Vietnam", promulgates a "provisional constitutional act" and sets up a committee to "draft the constitution of the Vietnamese nation".

December 29, 1955 Gen. Le Van Ty, Chief of staff of the South Vietnam army, reads an order of the day calling on the southern troops readily to "fill up the Ben Hai river" and "march to the North" (The Saigon press and radio carries out an intensive propaganda for the Ngo Dinh Diem "march to the North" policy)

*
* *

In 1955, parallel with the increase of the military personnel in the Military Aid Advisory Group (M.A.A G.) the sending of the Michigan State University (M S U.) to the South to help the Diem administration mainly in secret police matters, and the continuous introduction of American weapons into South Vietnam U.S. imperialism and the Ngo Dinh Diem administration frenziedly launched terrorist raids on the people (campaigns of Freedom, Liberation, Phan Chu Trinh, Dinh Tien Hoang, etc.) Early in 1955, Diem promulgated a so-called "Agrarian Reform" with such deceptive slogans as "distribute land to the peasants", "give property to the proletarians", "down with feudalism and colonialism". The United States sent to Diem an advisor, Ladejinsky, who had many experiences in helping Chiang Kai-shek work out his "agrarian reform" in Taiwan. In essence, Diem's "agrarian reform" in 1955 and the following years was aimed at helping the landlords wrest back the land distributed to the peasants during the anti-French Resistance and exploit the peasants more atrociously

Following are some movements waged by the South Vietnam people against the U S.-Diem clique in 1954

— The movement for the re-establishment of normal relations between North and South rose up after the February 4, 1955 statement of the Government of the D R V Since the end of August 1955, in nearly all the provinces of South Vietnam, strikes broke out one after the other, demanding a consultative conference about general elections

— The movement to oppose the "referendum" aimed at pitchforking Diem "President" and boycott the elections to the South Vietnam "National Assembly"

— The movement to oppose the forcible house removal under the cloak of "city-clearing" and demand improvement of the Saigon-Cholon people's living standard

— The movement to relieve the hunger-stricken inhabitants of Thua Thien and South Quang Tri after the big 1955 floods

— The movement to relieve the victims of the clash between the Diem troops and those of the Binh Xuyen clique and religious sects.

— The struggle of the workers to demand improvement of living standard and oppose sack.

1956

Janurary 11, 1956 : Diem promulgates ordinance № 6 setting up concentration camps to jail those alleged as "dangerous for the national defence and public security".

January 23, 1956 : The Diem administration decides to organize separatist elections to the "National Assembly" of South Vietnam.

February 20, 1956 : Diem promulgates ordinance № 13 muzzling the press.

March 4, 1956 Election to the "National Assembly" of South Vietnam by violence and fraud.

April 11, 1956 The Diem administration sends a memorandum to the British Government reiterating its standpoint of non recognition of the Geneva Agreement

April 28, 1956 Complete withdrawal of the French expeditionary corps from South Vietnam.

May 1, 1956 : Big meeting and demonstration in Saigon of 200,000 people from various strata (workers, labouring people, pressmen, writers, artistes, pupils, teachers, many capitalists, officials and even Diem's armymen and policemen). The slogans read end unemployment, extend the system of family allowance to workers of private enterprises, carry out an agrarian reform beneficial to the peasants , restrict the importation of foreign goods ; help the native capitalists develop national industry ; freedom of the press , long live peace, down with war , national reunification by peaceful means

July 2, 1956   The South Vietnam "National Assembly" sanctions the "constitution" for South Vietnam

*
* *

In 1956, the United States introduced into South Vietnam hundreds of military personnel under the disguise of "Temporary Equipment Recovery Mission" bringing the total amount of American military personnel in South Vietnam to nearly 2,000 as compared with 200 at the signing of the Geneva Agreements Moreover, by 1956, the effectives of the South Vietnam army built up by the United States reached 150,000 comprising several divisions of infantry, paratroopers and marines, not to mention the security forces and militia tens of thousands strong.

With these forces, the U.S -Diemists stepped up their "campaigns of indictment and extermination of Communists" to round up patriots in South Vietnam However, the major aim of the United States in building the South Vietnam army on a large scale was to "march to the North".

1957

January 4, 1957   Georges Chaffard, special correspondent of the French paper *Le Monde* in Saigon writes about the role of the U.S. advisers in South Vietnam as follows

"...When Gen. O'Daniel was presiding over the training of the Vietnamese army, it sometimes happened that he thumped the table, shouting "who pays ?" in order to force his views on doubting allies. The Vietnamese asked for a break in the sitting to confer together, then came back to announce their acceptance"

May 13, 1957 · During his visit to the United States, Ngo Dinh Diem states : "I am confident that we can hold on long enough to wait for the S.E.A.T.O. forces to help us. A Communist aggression can be checked by a similar co-operation between the South Vietnamese forces and those of S.E.A.T.O.".

On the same occasion, Diem shamelessly declares "The frontier of the United States extends to the 17 th parallel, the boundary between South and North Vietnam."

July 18, 1957 . Premier Pham Van Dong of the Government of the D.R.V. sends a note to Ngo Dinh Diem, once again proposing a consultative conference between the two zones to discuss about the general elections to reunify the country and pending that, the re-establishment of normal relations between the two zones.

August 9, 1957 Diem signs an ordinance to build the Saigon-Bien Hoa autobahn, 32 km long, 100m wide, with a bare stretch of 950 m wide on each side. In fact this is a gigantic airfield accessible to heavy strategic planes.

November 25, 1957 U.S. Vice-Admiral Beakley declares in Saigon that the U.S. Seventh Fleet would be ready for an offensive by all "defensive" acts required by the S E A.T.O. bloc or ordered by President Eisenhower.

November 30, 1957 . According to U.P.I at a meeting of the S.E A.T O. bloc at Baguio (Philippines) late in November 1957, Australian Gen. William Worth, its acting Secretary General, states that "The Republic of Vietnam, which has sent three observers to the Conference, is considered as the country which will most probably become the ninth member of the alliance."

*
* *

In 1957, the U.S.-Diem began implementing a two-year plan (1957-1958) to build a network of strategic roads. These link the military bases in the plains with the High Plateaux, one of the main U S strategic bases in South-East Asia. This system of military roads would go through Laos and reach Thailand in order to perfect a network of strategic communication lines to help the U S imperialists in their war preparations.

Moreover, early in 1957 (April 1957), Diem put forward the policy of setting up "agricultural settlements", and regarded it as a "state policy" on a par with that of "indictment of Communists". In truth, the "agricultural settlements" only aimed at serving the policy of U.S investment, exploitation, war preparation and suppression of the South Vietnam people's struggle. Nearly all the "agricultural settlements" were located in fertile zones in the former Resistance bases in the jungle, especially in the strategically important Western Plateaux. To serve the "state policy of indictment of Communists", the U.S.-Diemists advocated the setting up of a safe corridor from Pleiku, Kontum, and Ban Me Thuot, to the Plain of Reeds and Ca Mau The "agricultural settlements" constituted the vital positions of this corridor manned by strong garrisons under the command of Diem's officers. (In 1957 they were defended by 7,000 soldiers). Leland Barrows, head of the U S. operations mission in Saigon (U S O M) clearly said that "agricultural settlements" had to be turned into "positions encircling the Viet Cong" (after the Saigon paper Chan Hung Kinh Te — Economic Rehabilitation — of June 19, 1958).

Up to 1957, the South Vietnam economy was more and more subservient to U S imperialism Through the channel of "aid", U S. imperialism gradually took in hand the levers of the South Vietnam economy, turning the South into an outlet for the surplus goods of the United States and its camp. At a press conference in Saigon in April 1957, Ngo Dinh Nhu — Diem's brother and adviser — had to admit that "Vietnam has never been consulted about the goods it needs It has to consume all kinds of goods or to accept any product of any country."

In 1957, the South Vietnam people's struggle against the U.S.-Diemists was rampant and took on various forms

— Movement to oppose U.S aid and to build an independent economy,

— Movement to oppose city clearing, house eviction, transfer of population involving hundreds of thousands of townsfolk

— Movement to oppose taxes put up by separate sections or many strata of people,

— Movement to oppose pressganging into the army On the other hand, since 1957, with the impetus of the former period, the South Vietnam people's struggle against the U.S - Diem policy of "indictment of Communists" has been grim and fierce In the same year 1957, as the U S.-Diemists exerted themselves to enforce their "agrarian reform", the South Vietnam peasants' struggle to preserve their land became also more stubborn to such an extent that at the Conference on "agrarian reform" (October 1957) attended by U.S. "advisers", the Diem administration had to admit that "the agrarian reform is a fiasco".

1958

March 7, 1958 the Government of the D.R.V sends a note to the Diem administration pointing out the danger of the policy of aggression and enslavement by U.S. imperialism and proposing that the two zones would appoint delegates to discuss the measures rapidly to bring about peaceful national reunification on the basis of mutual understanding and compromise.

March 27, 1958 : At a meeting of the "Labour and Personalism" party, Ngo Dinh Nhu acknowledges the U S -Diem failure in the policy of "indictment of Communists"

April 26, 1958 In face of the energetic support to the note dated March 7, 1958 of the Government of the D.R.V proposing that both zones would reduce their army effectives and exchange trade with each other, the new administration had to issue a declaration in which mention is made of peace and reunification but also of preconditions to the sole effect of putting off national reunification, such as demanding of the North to reduce its army effectives first (while the U S -Diemists are increasing their military strength in the South), to let people evacuate to the South (while they persist in their opposition to re-establish normal relations between the two zones)..

May 1, 1958 . a huge demonstration is held in Saigon-Cholon by half a million people of all walks of life, with slogans demanding to solve the problem of unemployment for the workers, promote industry, secure job for the toilers , radically to carry out rational reduction of land rent, to fully apply the slogan "land to the tillers" , to peacefully reunify the country

May 14, 1958 · Despite the protest of the Polish delegation, the Indian and Canadian delegates of the International Commission for Control and Supervision sanction by a majority vote a resolution allowing the U.S imperialists and Ngo Dinh Diem to introduce American war material into South Vietnam on the ground that they are to replace the war material the French troops took with them at their departure from South Vietnam in April 1956.

December 1, 1958   the U.S.-Diem clique massacres the patriots detained in Phu Loi concentration camp (Thu Dau Mot) among 6,000 people poisoned at a time, over 1,000 meet with death instantaneously ; the survivors who try to cry for help are shot dead. This crime has caused a strong emotion among progressive mankind

December 22, 1958 the D.R V. government send to the South Vietnam administration a note pointing out, in substance that the deadlock which prevails in the life of the South Vietnam people is due to the U.S. imperialists' intervention , it suggests that a meeting between the authorities of both zones be convened to discuss and conclude an agreement on the problems most indispensable to the inhabitants of both zones and to create favourable conditions for the peaceful reunification of the country

*

*   *

During 1958 the U.S.-Diem clique continued to launch large-scale raids. To step up military activities, in 1958, the South Vietnam budget earmarked 64 per cent for military expenditure, not including the credit reserved for communications and public works whose main task is to build airbases, naval bases and strategic roads. The people's struggle began to shake the rank of the Diem clique. Many a time in 1958, Diem had to carry out purges within his rank, replacing 17 chiefs of province at a time, sacking thousands of officials in Saigon and Hue and dismissing 1,500 officers and non-commissioned officers and 500 men of the police and security service

In 1958, the struggle waged by the South Vietnam people against the U.S - Diem clique was marked by

--- the movement in support of the note of March 7, 1958 of the government of the D,R V

--- the campaign against U S. aid and for the establishment of an independent economy (already bubbling in 1957 but spreading particularly in 1958 while it was facing a crisis caused by the U S in the middle of 1958 out of 15,038 weaving looms, there were 10,527 which came to a stanstill at the end of the year, 10,000 sugar mills stopped working, 80 per cent of weavers and 100,000 workers and peasants of the sugar branch were jobless)

Other movements such as those demanding improvement of the livelihood, democratic liberties, the fighting against eviction of houses and concentration of people, against forced conscription of labour and pressganging into the army, against taxation, continued to spread to many localities In 1959 the U.S. - Diem regime began to face a serious crisis

1959

February 1959 in most provinces of South Vietnam, the inhabitants hold meetings and demonstrations, wear mourning, denounce the U.S. Diem clique as responsible for the massacre at Phu Loi Pagodas and temples hold requiem masses for the patriots killed in this concentration camp

March 1959 At the beginning of this month, Ngo Dinh Diem declares South Vietnam in a state of war Implementing this policy the "National Revolution", semi-official organ of the

93

Diem-Nhu brothers, puts forth the slogan "Annihilate the Viet Cong mercilessly, annihilate them as they are not human beings, annihilate them as in a state of war"; this paper also maps out a plan called "oil-stain plan" to merge all military and para-military forces in one bloc having concerted action according to a plan and placed under the command of a central organ. This is a plan to carry out mopping-up operations uninterruptedly in order to arrest and kill the patriots

April 1959. The minority peoples of the Western Plateaux (Central Vietnam) herded in "agricultural settlements" struggle to return to their native villages.

May 1, 1959 More than 210,000 workers and inhabitants of Saigon hold meetings and demonstrations on May Day.

May 6, 1959 The Diem authorities promulgate the fascist law 10-59 and use a special military court, and a special procedure to terrorize all people who stand against them and the U.S. (the accused can be sentenced to death or at least to life imprisonment even though there are no evidences or the crime is only attempted).

July 1959 The U.S-Diem clique puts forth the policy of setting up "prosperity zones", a new form of concentration camps, to bring the South Vietnam peasants under their control, and to curb the peasants' movement of struggle against the U.S.-Diem's cruel oppression and exploitation.

August 25, 1959 The Diem administration makes known the "policy towards ex-resistance members", by which it divides the members of the 1945-1954 resistance into two categories the first category groups all those who are recognized as ex-resistance members, and the second all those who are not recognized as such. Those of the second category are considered outlaws This is a deceitful scheme by which on the one hand the Diem authorities also recognize the role of the resistance members, but on the other, — and this is the main point — they want to differentiate between the South Vietnam people in order to faci-litate the work of accusation by special military courts

August 30, 1959 Ngo Dinh Diem stages the election to the "National Assembly", second legislature, by means of repression and cheating, with a view to bringing his obedient lackeys in this "assembly" and discard those who are not to his liking

*

* *

Since the signing of the Geneva Agreements on Indo-China in 1954 until the end of 1959, the South Vietnam authorities took part in six conferences and seven military manoeuvres of the S E.A.T.O. military bloc. From 1955 to 1959, American "aids" to the Diem administration amounted to the lumpsum of over one billion dollars, of which military aids accounted for over 700 million At the end of 1959, the Diem authorities shipped also a great quantity of weapons from Malaya to South Vietnam and applied the Malayan "anti-communist" experiences

Throughout 1959, the U.S.-Diem clique actively carried out the "oil-stain plan" by fiercely raiding large areas from Camau cape to the demilitarized zone, passing through the Western Plateaux. In some raids the U.S -Diem clique used as many as 15,000 soldiers propped up by aircraft Their aim is to capture the patriots either to kill them on the spot or to summon them before special military courts and to coerce the population to live in "prosperity zones".

While until the middle of 1959, the Diem administration was temporarily consolidated and kept the initiative in attack, from mid-1959 onward, the political situation of South Vietnam has undergone important changes The movement of struggle of the South Vietnam people against the U S -Diem's despotic domination has developed most powerfully and broadly and with it ended the stabilization of the U.S -Diem regime, and began a permanent crisis. In the countryside, meetings and demonstrations have taken place one after the other involving from some hundreds to some thousands of people, and spreading to whole villages, districts or provinces Sometimes the demonstrators marched to district-towns and struggled directly against the Diem administration for the destruction of "prosperity zones" rescission of law 10-59, ending of terrorist raids and of conscription of labour and soldiers, and reduction of taxes and corvées. A most important point is that in face of the cruel repression by the U S.-Diem clique the South Vietnam people continued their political struggles, and combined political struggles with armed struggles, manufactured weapons and seized them from the enemy, to protect their lives and property

1960

March 1960. At the end of March 1960, 4,000 inhabitants of Cai Be district (My Tho province) destroy a "prosperity zone"

April, 29, 1960 The I.C sanctions by a majority vote - strongly opposed by the Polish delegate — the resolution by which the Diem administration is allowed to introduce more U S military personnel into South Vietnam

April 1960. 600 enemy soldiers of "the Quang Trung training Centre" desert and join the people's side

May 1960: Hundreds of thousands of northern people, coerced to go South, now living in the Plain of Reeds, struggle against terrorism, exploitation and pressganging and demand to return to the North.

June 1960 Tens of thousands of minority people of the Western Plateaux rise against the enemy for having destroyed crops, set up "Prosperity zones", built strategic roads and established military bases This struggle receives the support of the minority soldiers.

A South Vietnam regiment stationed in the southernmost part of Central Vietnam protest against orders to raid the people of Quang Ngai province.

July 20, 1960 In Central South Vietnam, 600,000 people from 400 villages out of 505 villages, organize over 500 meetings and hundreds of demonstrations, distribute leaflets, hang slogans and hoist flags in various rural regions, district-towns, urban centres and "prosperity zones" and demand . abrogation of law 10-59, an end to terrorism and massacres, order and security for the population , dismantling of "prosperity zones" and concentration camps, the ousting of M.A.A.G. from South Vietnam and the overthrow of the Ngo Dinh Diem regime.

September 11, 1960 · More than 1,000 teachers and students and their parents meet in Saigon, demanding to use the Vietnamese language as vehicle for teaching in higher education establishments.

September 20, 1960 : 2,800 monks and 20,000 people of Tra Vinh province march to the provincial town demanding freedom of belief, and order and security for the population.

October 10, 1960 · 9,000 inhabitants of Binh Thuan and Ninh Thuan provinces demolish many "prosperity zones" and return to their native villages.

October 19, 1960 · Ngo Dinh Diem proceeds to what is called reshuffle of his cabinet (the 12th since his coming into office to the end of 1960. During these reshuffles he sacked 35 ministers, dismissed one third of the total number of his generals and about 30 majors and colonels. In 1960 alone, he changed or dismissed 18 heads of province, 30 deputy heads of province and many ministers)

November 11, 1960 A coup d'état to overthrow Ngo Dinh Diem's regime is engineered in Saigon by a section of Diem's army under the command of Colonel Nguyen Chanh Thi and Major Vuong Van Dong. Phan Quang Dan, a pro-American who is however looked askance by Ngo Dinh Diem, is "political counsellor" of the coupmen. The putsch fails owing to lack of determination of the instigators and especially to their non-reliance on the people Despite its failure, the coup testifies to the great rottenness of the Diem regime and reveals that, on seeing that Diem is not up to his task of repressing the people, some American organs want to have him replaced Therefrom contradictions between the U.S imperialists and Ngo Dinh Diem begin to arise.

While the coup is unfolding, over 5,000 people of Saigon city demonstrate against the Diem administration and demand the setting up of a unified national democratic administration, and expulsion of the U.S imperialists from South Vietnam. Diem's troops and the coup's armymen shoot at the demonstrators causing many casualties

November 1960 . 1 5 million people from 450 villages in South Central Vietnam hold 1,500 meetings and demonstrations to demand abrogation of fascist law 10-59, dissolution of "prosperity zones", and resignation of Ngo Dinh Diem.. The people directly struggle against the heads of province and district and post commanders.

December 1960 · 100,000 people of the Eastern part of Nam Bo (South Vietnam) demonstrate against the U.S.-Diem clique.

December 20, 1960   The South Vietnam Liberation National Front is founded in a people-controlled region of Nam Bo. The Front makes known its manifesto and programme of action aiming at uniting all the sections of the population, all nationalities, religions, patriotic personalities, to overthrow the U.S.-Diem clique, set up a unified national democratic government to achieve independence, peace, neutrality freedom and democracy and advance toward national reunification

*

*   *

At the end of 1960, the M.A A.G staff numbered 3,000 including 3 generals. This American mission was organized with all its sections :   military   operations,   commissariat,   psychological warfare, intelligence service, etc. and has its men from Ngo Dinh Diem's Ministry of National Defence to military sectors and units, and in fact, it has become a supreme command lording it over Diem's Ministry of National Defence. M.A.A.G.'s men directly control and supervise the carrying out of U.S. military plans in South Vietnam, from the building up of the army to the construction of military bases and strategic roads

According to Saigon press report, until the end of 1960, the U.S. imperialists had built the South Vietnam army into a force divided as follows .

Regular army	150,000 men,
Bao An (Defence of security)	60,000 —
Police and security	45,000 —
Dan Ve (People's self defence)	100,000 —

During that period there were in the South 57 airbases and military airfields (as against 6 military airbases existing in South Vietnam at the restoration of peace in 1954. The U.S. imperialists paid particular attention to building the Tan Son Nhut airfield into a strategic airbase which, together with Don Muang in Thailand and Clarkfield in the Philippines, constitutes a system of strategic airbases of the U.S.A. in South-East Asia. The Western Plateaux (Central Vietnam) attract the attention of the U.S. imperialists who build there many airfields including the "peace" airfield at Banmethout which can receive heavy jet planes. Such large airfields as Tan Son Nhut, Nha Trang, Da Nang are placed under the direct command of U.S. air advisers.

Naval bases and supplying bases were urgently built by the U.S.-Diem clique (the naval bases of Nha Be and Da Nang have been expanded and modernized to receive big warships)

Up to 1960, American war material was introduced into South Vietnam at a very quick tempo. From the second half of 1954 to 1957, the total number of shippings amounted to 211 only while there were

114 shippings in	1958
226	—	1959
235	—	1960

Each shipping varied between some hundred tons to some thousand tons.

In 1960, the U.S.-Diem clique frenziedly terrorized the people by launching 2,185 big and small raids ; in some of them they used as much as one division ; in hundreds of others, their force amounted from one to nine battalions. American advisers directly commanded these raids together with Diem's officers. Where there are military operations, there special military courts are set up (in virtue of law 10-59) dragging with them the guillotine. Many evil doers of the Diem's army slaughtered people and disembowelled the civilians to eat their livers and galls.

However, the stubborn struggle of the people landed the Diem administration in a defensive position and caused them continual setbacks and crises. The rural authority of the Diem administration collapsed and in these regions the people manage their own affairs. Besides, the contradictions between Ngo Dinh Diem and the religious sects and political parties have become so acute that suspicion prevailed in the puppet administration and Diem could rely on nobody and really became a despot grasping all power in his hand.

1961

February 5, 1961 . UPI reports that the Malayan authorities ship to South Vietnam 45,707 rifles, over 10,000 small arms, 346 armoured cars, 241 small vehicles and 206 armoured vehicles.

February 15, 1961 : the South Vietnam people's self-defence armed forces merge into the South Vietnam Liberation army and are recognized as a member of the South Vietnam Liberation National Front,

March 24, 1961 . the New York Times reports that South Vietnam is considered as the key position for anti-communist defence in South-East Asia and has become an experimental ground for the American troops to test new tactics on guerilla warfare in tropical jungles and mountains.

April 9, 1961 the farcical election of the President and Vice-president (second legislature) is held in South Vietnam.

May 6, 1961 the French paper "Liberation" quotes Dean Rusk as saying about the policy of U.S. President Kennedy, that, "the President has authorized an increase of military aid to the Republic of Vietnam, the importance of which I am not in a position to reveal".

May 11, 1961. U.S. Vice President L. Johnson comes to Saigon, with a 15-point letter from Kennedy to Ngo Dinh Diem, the main points are :

— strengthening the security force of South Vietnam and using it to expand the regular army of South Vietnam ,

— Sending missions of U.S military advisers to help in the training of self-defence units at hamlet level ;

— Granting financial aids to increase the regular army by 20,000 men.

— Special training of regular army units in guerilla warfare.

— Sending American engineering corps to repair the bridges destroyed or damaged by the guerillas and to build roads and airfields.

May 13, 1961 : Release of the Johnson-Diem communiqué containing 8 points which are, in substance, the concretization of the plan elaborated by Kennedy in his letter to Diem.

June 11, 1961. Arrival in Saigon of the first batch of U.S. "advisers" on anti-guerilla warfare, under the command of major Williams.

June 19, 1961 : A joint economic and military mission headed by E. Staley arrives in Saigon. Upon his return to the U.S.A., Staley has made important suggestions, which have been approved by the White House and become the programme of action of the U.S.A. in South Vietnam, This plan known under the "Staley Plan" can be summarized in three steps ·

Step 1 : Pacification of South Vietnam within eighteen months and establishment of bases in North Vietnam.

Step 2 : Economic restoration and strengthening of the South Vietnam army, stepping up of sabotage activities in North Vietnam.

Step 3 Development of South Vietnam's economy and attack on North Vietnam.

July 2, 1961 : An aircraft C. 47 sent by the U.S. - Diem clique to airdrop commandos in North Vietnam is shot down at Ninh Binh by an anti-aircraft unit of the V.P.A.

July 22, 1961 Ngo Dinh Diem signs a decree pressganging public servants, doctors and pharmacists into the army, and compelling all men from 20 to 33, partially graduated from baccalaureate or having a corresponding diploma, to attend an officer-training course.

October 3, 1961 . Kennedy discusses the question of sending American troops to South Vietnam with his Defence Secretary McNamara, Gen Lemnitzer, Chairman of Joint Chiefs of Staff, Gen. M. Taylor, his personal adviser, and other high-ranking officers.

October 18, 1961 . Kennedy sends Taylor to Saigon. Ngo Dinh Diem promulgates a decree declaring the whole of South Vietnam in a state of emergency (the decree is said to have been signed on October 15.)

November 3, 1961 : Ngo Dinh Diem signs a decree submitting South Vietnamese women to para-military training.

November 15, 1961 . U.S. National Security Council sanctions Taylor's proposals amending the Staley plan and carrying out the first step of armed aggression against South Vietnam.

To carry out the Staley-Taylor plan, Nolting U.S. Ambassador to Saigon, and Ngo Dinh Diem hold a three-week discussion in November 1961, after which, U.S. armaments, military personnel and combat units are very urgently introduced into South Vietnam on a scale unknown up to that time.

December 16, 1961 : McNamara, Lemnitzer and Harry Felt, commander-in-chief of U.S. Pacific forces, Nolting, etc., meet in Honolulu to consider the carrying out of the military plan in South Vietnam.

*

* *

In 1961, parallel with mopping-up operations — 20,000 raids of which 400 were of large-scale — U.S.-Diem's airplanes sprayed toxic chemicals over many localities in South Vietnam.

According to investigations made by the South Vietnam Liberation Red Cross Society, besides the products 2-4D and 2-4-5T used in a strong dose, the U.S.-Diem clique also sprayed white arsenic, alcali arsenites, alcate earth, calcic cyanamide, metallic arsenate, 2-4 dinitriphenol DNP, and dinitro-orthocresol DNC. Rejecting the execrable lies of the U.S. Government and its henchmen in South Vietnam that these chemicals are not dangerous to men and animals, such American papers as the New Republic and the Gazette and Daily, and many scientists such as Lord Bertrand Russel and the naturalist Rachel Careon, have affirmed that these products are not only harmful to vegetation but also to men and animals alike

Besides, applying the experiences of the British colonialists in Malaya, as early as July 1961, the U.S.-Diem clique set up, in some localities on an experimental basis, new-type concentration camps called "strategic hamlets" in the hope of oppressing the South Vietnam people and separating them from the guerillas in order to annihilate them both more easily. Usually a "strategic hamlet" is built with a surrounding fence of bamboos of wooden spikes from 2 to 2.5 metres high ; inside is another fence of barbed wire. Between these two fences lies a field of spikes and mines. Behind the barbed wire is a moat, 3 metres wide and 1.5 metres deep, also bristling with spikes. Further inside is an earth wall 1.5 metres high defended here and there by concrete blockhouses. In the middle of the hamlet are various offices of the hamlet managing board, of the youth and "Republican" women. The headquarters is built in the form of a military post linked to the blockhouse and watch towers by underground trenches and communication trenches — the hamlet inmates are compelled to take each a plastic identity card with fingerprints and photo on. Going in and out of the strategic hamlet is subject to time regulation and control. To prevent any possible food supply to the guerillas, the U.S. imperialists and their henchmen compel the inmates to concentrate their paddy and other foodstuffs and to take back each time just what is needed for their daily ration.

*

With the founding of the South Vietnam Liberation National Front at the end of 1960 and the beginning of 1961, the Front organizations covered the length and breadth of South Vietnam. One after the other, various organs, patriotic organizations and parties in the South joined the Front of their free will to fight for the carrying out of the Front's platform Under the leadership of the South Vietnam Liberation National Front, during the first half of 1961 alone, nearly 3 million people struggled directly against the terror of the enemy, claimed democratic liberties, demanded the setting up of a united democratic national government, and opposed U.S. intervention in South Vietnam; in the South, the number of people who fought collectively many times against the oppression of the enemy totalled 17 million, these struggles shook and shattered the Diem administrative machinery in many villages; in the mountain regions of South Central Vietnam the administration collapsed in 4,400 hamlets out of 4,700 hamlets. In the plains of South Central Vietnam, the inhabitants rose up powerfully and shattered the U.S.-sponsored administration in many localities, throwing the officials in greater confusion; desertion in the army increased; in some places the deserters shot at their commanders before joining the Liberation troops with their weapons; many prosperity zones were destroyed, tens of thousands of people were liberated and returned to their native places.

Since mid-1961, the struggle has become fiercer owing to direct armed aggression by the U.S. imperialists with their Staley-Taylor plan. The South Vietnam Liberation National Front called on all the South Vietnam people to unite for the defence of the vital interests of the Fatherland so as to thwart the aggressive scheme of the U.S. imperialists, overthrow the rotten Ngo Dinh Diem regime and pave the way for the peaceful reunification of the country.

In 1961, the South Vietnam people and Liberation army annihilated, captured and wounded over 32,000 enemy troops, including 30 Americans, and took 7,300 arms of all descriptions. Besides more than 17,000 soldiers deserted the puppet army.

1962

January 1, 1962: the South Vietnam Revolutionary People's Party is founded and joins the South Vietnam Liberation National Front. It declares to be the "Party of the working class and toiling people of South Vietnam and at the same time the Party of all patriotic people of South Vietnam"; it sets for itself the task "to unite and lead the working class, peasants, toiling people and all the people of South Vietnam, in their struggle to overthrow the domination of imperialism and feudalism, now U.S. imperialism and the Ngo Dinh Diem clique, quislings of the U.S.; to liberate South Vietnam, set up a broad united national democratic power, to achieve national independence, freedom and democracy, to improve the people's livelihood, give land to the tillers, promote industry and trade, develop culture and education, improve the people's material life by supplying them sufficiently with food and clothing, pave the way for peaceful reunification of the country and contribute to the defence of world peace."

January 10, 1962. a British government's delegation of experts of administrative affairs and police comes to Saigon. It is headed by Gen. G. K. Thompson, former permanent secretary for national defence of Malaya, commander of the anti-guerilla war in Malaya. The mission is entrusted with the task of helping the U.S.-sponsored puppet administration in South Vietnam in experiences and applying them in the repression of the patriotic movement of the South Vietnam people.

January 17, 1962· The Provisional Central Committee of the South Vietnam Liberation National Front promulgates 10 immediate policies of the Front, the first 4 points of which are:

1. To respect the Geneva Agreements, to demand the U.S. imperialists to stop all armed aggression, withdraw weapons, military advisers and G.I.s from South Vietnam, and cancel the Staley-Taylor-Nolting plan.

2. To immediately restore peace in South Vietnam, put an end to the war against the people, stop terror, repression, arrests and massacres of the people, guarantee order and security for the people.

3. To carry out democratic liberties, give all parties and sects freedom of establishment and action, freedom of the press and publication, freedom of cult for all religions, etc. All parties shall be free to present candidates to stand for elections to the National Assembly and other institutions.

4. To dissolve the National Assembly and cancel the existing constitution owing to its illegal character, to elect a new National Assembly and draft a new constitution in a democratic manner

February 8, 1962 : The U.S. Defence Department officially issues a communiqué establishing in Saigon an organ called Military Aid Command (M.A.C.) under Gen. P.D. Harkins.

February 16, 1962 · The South Vietnam Liberation National Front holds its first Congress from February 16 to March 3, 1962 and issued a statement calling for a biggest and broadest rally of all forces and elements of good will among the people to concentrate their strength for staying the hands of a ferocious enemy, the U.S. imperialist aggressors and their henchmen, the Ngo Dinh Diem ruling clique. The Congress elects the official Central Committee of the Front which consists of 52 members (of this number, 21 seats are reserved for mass organizations, political parties, and groups of patriotic personalities who will eventually join the Front) under the chairmanship of Lawyer Nguyen Huu Tho.

February 18, 1962 : The Government of the D.R.V. issues a statement vehemently to protest against U.S. aggressive military activities which have become most serious with the establishment of the M.A.C.

February 27, 1962 . Two fighters of the Air Force of the South Vietnam administration strafe and bomb the Independence Palace of Ngo Dinh Diem who is able to escape thanks to the protection of an underground blockhouse.

May 23, 1962 : Ngo Dinh Diem's law court tries Professor Le Quang Vinh and 11 students and youths on account of their anti-U.S activities Le Quang Vinh and 3 other students are sentenced to death, the rest to hard labour imprisonment. In face of this fascist verdict, Le Quang Vinh vehemently says : "I regret that I could not kill the chieftain of the aggressors", and shouts . "Down with Ngo Dinh Diem ! Down with the fascist laws !"

July 20, 1962 : The South Vietnam Liberation National Front puts forth four emergency policies for national salvation on the occasion of the 8th anniversary of the signing of the Geneva Agreements on Indo-China. The contents of these policies are aimed at demanding the U.S. imperialists to put an end to their aggressive activities, withdraw their troops from South Vietnam for the South Vietnam people to decide their own affairs by themselves, demanding the U.S. imperialists and their henchmen to stop their acts of terrorism and repression, and the massacre of people ; demanding the dismantling of "strategic hamlets", the establishment of a national democratic coalition government and the ensuing holding of a free general election to a new National Assembly, the enforcement of various democratic freedoms, etc., and demanding that South Vietnam should practise a foreign policy of genuine peace and neutrality.

August, 3, 1962 : An Australian Military mission consisting of 30 officers under Col. Frank P. Serong arrives in Saigon to combine their action with that of the U.S. military "advisers" in South Vietnam

October 19. 1962 : A Front's delegation led by Professor Nguyen Van Hieu visits North Vietnam, bringing to 17 million North Vietnamese people, the expression of "an unshakable heart, a "Brass Wall" will, a monolithic solidarity and a determination to fight and to win" of their 14 million South Vietnam kith-and-kin.

November 23, 1962 : The New York Herald Tribune writes .
"The U.S. is deeply involved in the biggest "secret" war in its history. Never have so many U.S. military-men been involved in a combat area without a formal program to inform the public

about what is happening. It is a war fought without official public reports on the number of troops involved nor the amount of money and equipment being poured in."

December 12, 1962 · President Kennedy acknowledges at a press conference that in the anti-guerilla war in South Vietnam, the U.S.A. is being in a tunnel with no end in view.

*

* *

To speed up their armed aggression against South Vietnam, in 1962, the U S. imperialists held four meetings in Honolulu (February, March, July and October) under the chairmanship of Defence Secretary McNamara, with the participation of U.S. high-ranking officers. On May 9, 1962, McNamara held a meeting right in Saigon for the same purpose attended by A. Sylvester, U.S. Deputy. Secretary of Defence, Lyman Lemnitzer, Chairman of Joint chiefs-of-staff of th U S. Army, Harry Felt, Commander of the U S forces in the Pacific, Gen. Paul D. Harkins, and F. Nolting, U.S. ambassador to Saigon. In 1962 more than 30 missions including many U.S. high-ranking officers of all arms came to South Vietnam to inspect the activities of the U.S troops in this region.

Up to November 1962, the U.S. military personnel in South Vietnam amounted to 11,000 (as against 4,000 in 1962). To serve the U.S. special war in South Vietnam, the Ngo Dinh Diem administration strove to intensify the pressganging of soldiers at a rapid rate, and forced public servants and women to undergo military training.

Throughout 1962, the U.S.-Diem clique launched a series of large-scale mopping-up operations aimed at realizing the Staley-Taylor scheme of pacifying South Vietnam. Gen. Harkins and his staff were the authors of the plans of operations called "Sunrise", "Pacification of the West," Boondodge, etc. "Sunrise" was a large-scale operation dragging from March 23, 1962 to the end of 1962 with the participation of two divisions of regular forces supported by local armed forces, air force and artillery. In this operation, Defence Secretary McNamarra, Gen Lemnitzer and Harkins came in person to observe on the spot. In 1962, there were 27,000 small mopping-up operations and nearly 1,000 large mopping-up operations involving a battalion upward Besides mopping-up operations, the U.S. Diem clique used their airforce to drop explosive bombs, napalm bombs and gas-bombs, and to spray noxious chemicals to massacre the South Vietnam people, kill the cattle and destroy crops (on January 10, 1963, in summing up the U.S. "exploits" after one year of aggressive war in South Vietnam, Harkins openly said that in 1962 the U.S. troops had killed 30,000 persons, though this figure is far from the truth).

In the hope of gaining victory, the U S.A. introduced into South Vietnam a great quantity of new war material such as most up-to-date jet planes, helicopters (Flying Banana, HU.-1A, HU-1B, Mohawk equipped with rockets) and M. 113 amphibious armoured carriers, etc, and applied new tactics such as Flying Eagle, Use of amphibious carriers, etc.

In 1962, the U S-Diem clique also strove to carry out their plan of herding the population into "strategic hamlets" in the hope of concentrating by the end of 1962 10 million South Vietnam people into 16,332 "strategic hamlets" (South Vietnam has 17,000 villages and hamlets in all)

*

In response to the appeal of the South Vietnam Liberation National Front, the political struggle of the South Vietnam people in 1962 rose like a high tide shaking to the very root the U S.-sponsored puppet administration in South Vietnam. Take Ben Tre province for an example · Up to the beginning of 1962, 90 per cent of the land of this province was completely liberated. Within 50 days from April 1, 1962 to May 20, 1962, its people held 737 meetings, 280 demonstrations, 10,027 rallies in villages and hamlets to denounce US-Diem crimes, and organized 84 requiems for the repose of the victims' souls ; there were 2,794 contacts of the masses with the local administration compelling it to accept 15,000 claims, 211 petitions and other demands. The struggle of various strata of people in towns also rose up powerfully (the struggles of the workers against sacking, for wage lift and reduction of working hours, were sometimes very stubborn and took the form of strikes and occupation of enterprises. Pupils and students struggled for the use of the Vietnamese language as a vehicle in higher schools, for educational reforms, reduction of fees...). The tendency to peace and neutrality gained even militarymen and public servants of the South Vietnam administration.

In their armed struggle, the South Vietnam people also scored many big successes. In many fights against mopping-up operations, the South Vietnam Liberation Army destroyed whole enemy companies, in some case even whole battalions.

The year 1962 ended with the fiasco of the U.S.-Diem clique's plan of building "strategic hamlets".

In 1962, the South Vietnam Liberation Army and people.

— put out of action over 50,000 enemies (dead, wounded and captured) including 443 Americans, disbanded nearly 35,000 enemy troops, and captured thousands of weapons of every description ;

— shot down 64 airplanes, (for the greater part helicopters), and damaged over 100 helicopters ;

— derailed 18 trains, destroyed about 400 armoured carriers, trucks and other kinds of vehicles, and many boats, burnt more than 6 million litres of gasolene.

Till late 1962, the South Vietnam people

— destroyed over 2,600 out of the 3,700 "strategic hamlets" built by the U.S.-Diem clique. Among the destroyed "strategic hamlets", 320 were razed to the ground, 115 transformed into fighting villages against the U.S.-Diem clique, the rest were hamlets destroyed many times, some even over 30 times ;

— to free 9,082 villages from the oppression of the U.S.-Diem clique, completely liberated 4,441 others, that is about 76 per cent of the total number of villages in South Vietnam, with about 7 million inhabitants (50 per cent of the South Vietnam population).

*

In 1962, besides the visit of its delegation to North Vietnam, the South Vietnam Liberation National Front has seen its prestige raised with the visit of its delegation to a number of socialist countries and nationalist countries (People's China, the Soviet Union, the People's Democratic Republic of Korea, the German Democratic Republic, Czechoslovakia, Cuba, Indonesia) and with its participation in various international conference such as . the Conference of the International Organization of Journalists held in Hungary, the Conference of the World Federation of Democratic Youth held in Poland, the Conference of the International Union of Students held in Leningrad, the Afro-Asian Economic Seminar held in Colombo, the Conference of the Asian African Democratic Lawyers held in Konakry, etc..

1963

January 2, 1963 : The South Vietnam Liberation Army and people score a resounding victory at Ap Bac : 200 men of the Liberation Army together with the Ap Bac inhabitants (My Tho province) heroically oppose an enemy mopping-up operation. They completely smash the offensive of 2,000 US.-Diem troops under the American general R H York, annihilate 450 enemy troops, shoot down 6 airplanes including HU-1A jet planes, damage 11 others, burn 3 M. 113 amphibious cars, and sink a warship.

January 18, 1963 . A mission headed by Gen Earle G. Wheeler, Chief-of-Staff of U.S infantry and consisting of 5 generals, an admiral and 10 high-ranking officers representing various arms of the U.S Army come to Saigon. A F.P. reports that this is an American Military mission of unprecedented importance which comes on a visit to South Vietnam

February 1, 1963 Dean Rusk, U.S Secretary of State, declares at a press conference in Washington that there has never been such a hard, wearisome and discouraging expedition as that against the guerillas in South Vietnam.

February 15, 1963. The New York Herald Tribune writes that the relations between the U.S A. and the Ngo Dinh Diem administration have entered a new phase which is delicate and most critical.

March 1, 1963 · 62 American personalities and intellectuals write to Kennedy protesting against the U.S. war of aggression in South Vietnam

April 8, 1963. The Military Commission attached to the Central Committee of the South Vietnam Liberation National Front starts an "Ap Bac Emulation Movement to kill the Enemy and Score eats of Arms" for 1963

May 8, 1963 Ngo Dinh Diem forbids the Buddhist believers to hold a commemorative anniversary of Buddha's birthday on May 1st ; for this reason, on May 8, nearly ten thousand monks, nuns and Buddhists in Hue hold a meeting demanding freedom of belief, the right to fly the Buddhist flag and to celebrate the anniversary of Buddha's birthday. The U.S. Diem clique send police and security forces supported by armoured carriers equipped with 37mm guns, to repress most ruthlessly the empty-handed demonstrators, causing 12 killed and many wounded, not including hundreds arrested Since then, white terror prevailed throughout South Vietnam from Camau Cape to the 17th parallel. Hundreds of pagodas were surrounded by very thick barbed wire fences of the armed police force ; thousands of monks, nuns, Buddhists, pupils and students were arrested, tortured, imprisoned and exiled, and hundreds of people killed most pitilessly.

June 11, 1963 Superior Thich Quang Duc burns himself in Saigon to protest against the fascist repressive measures of the Ngo Dinh Diem administration against Buddhism

June 16, 1963 : 700,000 people hold a demonstration in Saigon-Cholon against the U.S.-Diem's terror and repression of Buddhists. Even public servants, high-ranking officers of the South Vietnam administration and army, a number of paratroopers and many Catholics also take part in the demonstration.

July 17, 1963. Dean Rusk declares that the U.S.A. has asked its allies, members of S.E.A.T.O., to redouble their efforts in order to put an end to the war against the guerillas in South Vietman.

July 17, 1963: 1,000 monks and nuns hold a demonstration from the Giac Minh Pagoda to the Xa Loi Pagoda (Saigon). Diem's police arrests hundreds of people. Many clashes take place between the demonstrators and the police, resulting in many wounded.

July 30, 1963 · 15,000 Buddhist believers hold a demonstration in Hue city. 15,000 Saigon people hold a requiem for the repose of Superior Thich Quang Duc's soul.

August 14, 1963: 15,000 American priests write to President Kennedy protesting against the aggressive war kindled by the U.S.A. in South Vietnam.

August 20, 1963: Ngo Dinh Diem enforces martial law throughout South Vietnam.

10,000 out of the 80,000 Hue people resolutely struggle to prevent thousands of Diem's troops crossing the Gia Hoi bridge in an attempt to destroy Dieu De Pagoda.

September 2, 1963: The contradiction between the U.S A. and Ngo Dinh Diem is ever sharper : The *Time of Vietnam* (Saigon) accuses C.I.A. for having spent from 10 to 24 million dollars to overthrow Ngo Dinh Diem at 11 p.m., August 27, 1963.

September 4, 1963: Walter Lipmann writes in the *New York Herald Tribune* that with regard to Diem, there are among the American political circles, two currents of opinions : one is to cut off aid until a group of generals overthrow Diem, and the other is to maintain Diem while compelling him to reshuffle his government.

September 7, 1963: According to a spokesman of the Press of the U S. State Department. President Kennedy's desire to reform the South Vietnam government, even to change a number of persons, remains unchanged.

October 8, 1963 The U.N.O decides to send a fact-finding mission to Saigon. The U S.A attempts to pave the way for the intervention of U.N.O in South Vietnam.

October 20, 1963. Opening in Hanoi of the meeting of the International Trade Union Committee for Solidarity with the Workers and People of South Vietnam This Conference points out "The struggle of the South Vietnam people against the aggression by the U.S imperialists, for national reunification, is an integral part of the struggle for national independence, world peace, democracy and freedom "

November 1, 1963. A group of officers headed by Gen Duong Van Minh stage a coup d'état overthrowing Ngo Dinh Diem. The Diem-Nhu brothers have tried to fly but are killed.

November 2, 1963 While Saigon still resounds with the gun-shots of the coup d'état, the *New York Herald Tribune* writes, "Despite the State Department's flat denial that the U.S. government is involved in the uprising, this revolt is our revolt "

November 6. 1963 The junta found a provisional government with Duong Van Minh as Chief of State and Nguyen Ngoc Tho (former vice-President of Diem's government) as Premier

November 8, 1963 The South Vietnam Liberation National Front issues a statement containing 6 most urgent demands to solve the South Vietnam serious situation.

1. Unconditionally to overthrow the whole of Ngo Dinh Diem's fascist regime,

2. To apply without delay a genuine broad democratic regime;

3 To put an end to U.S. aggression in South Vietnam;

4 To carry out the policy of independent democratic and rational economy in order to raise the people's living standard

5. Immediately to stop mopping-up operations, and massacres of the South Vietnam people

114

6 To progress toward negotiations between the interested parties in South Vietnam in order to come to a cease-fire and solve the important problems affecting the nation.

November 24, 1963 U.S. President Johnson calls on all U.S. government departments concerned with South Vietnam to pool their efforts and support the South Vietnam puppet administration against the "Viet Cong"

December 14, 1963 Dealing with the military setbacks of the U S A. and the Duong Van Minh group within a month after the overthrow of Ngo Dinh Diem, Reuter reports

"November was the bloodiest month this year in South Vietnam's guerilla war, and the most disastrous for the government side. The ratio of weapons lost during the month of November for example was about 1,500 against 455 or approximately ten government weapons conceded for every three captured from the Viet Cong. Viet Cong initiated incidents totalled 3,100 for the month, a high for the year One week in early November was the heaviest week for the year with 1,021 incidents..."

*

* *

To speed up their "special war" in South Vietnam, the U.S imperialists held in 1963 two meetings at Honolulu (May and November 1963) presided over by McNamara. In its issue of December 2, 1963 *Newsweek* revealed that at a meeting held in November the U.S. imperialists studied 140 maps relating to the topography of South Vietnam, minutely reconsidered the situation of 43 South Vietnam provinces, took stock of the report of Henry Cabot Lodge, U.S ambassador in Saigon, analysed the South Vietnam political situation, and then issued a 2,000-word communiqué, expressing their "optimism" with regard to the South Vietnam situation.

Up to September 1963, as admitted by late President Kennedy, the number of U S officers and men taking part in the war in South Vietnam rose up to 25,000. In 1963, over 40 missions including nearly all topmost officers of U.S. arms and various

115

branches of U.S. Defence Department, came to Saigon. McNamara himself came to South Vietnam twice within three months (September 24 and December 20, 1963) to study the situation on the spot. The number of mopping-up operations launched by the U.S. imperialists and their henchmen reached 37,000 in 1963, involving from one compagny to one division. A number of these large-scale mopping-ups bore such names as Love's Wave, Virtue's Triumph, Blazing Fire, Strong Wind, Sea-gull, etc.

*

In 1963, parallel with the seething struggle in the countryside against mopping-up operations, terror, spraying of noxious chemicals, concentration of people into "strategic hamlets", the political struggle of various strata of people in South Vietnam towns also developed on a scale and in a form never known before. Out of tens of millions of demonstrators participating in the political struggle 6 million were in Saigon, Hue and other towns. Most outstanding was the struggle of the Buddhists for freedom of belief warmly supported by the broad masses of people ; it was one of the factors accelerating the complete collapse of Ngo Dinh Diem's nepotic dictatorship.

After the resounding Ap Bac victory the South Vietnam Liberation Army and people won many successes at Plei M'rong (Gia Lai province), Bien Nhi (Ca Mau province), Giong Trom (Ben Tre province), Tan Tru (Cho Lon province), Cho Gao (My Tho province), Tan Nien Dong — Tan Nien Tay (Go Cong province), Dam Doi — Cai Nuoc (Ca Mau province), Soc Trang, Loc Ninh (Rach Gia province), Tan Phu (Ca Mau province), Hiep Hoa (Cho Lon province), Cha La (Ca Mau province)... These successes inflicted heavy losses upon the U.S. imperialists and their henchmen. The growth of the South Vietnam Liberation army in the armed struggle in 1963 was described by Mr Tran Nam Trung representing the Military Commission attached to the South Vietnam Liberation National Front at its Second Congress held early in 1964 as follows, "If two years ago, in the fight against a mopping-up operation, our army and people could wipe out only 30 or 40 enemy troops, and shoot down one or

116

two planes, today we can smash large-scale mopping-up operations ten times and even twenty times stronger, put out of action
400 or 500 enemy troops, down or damage 10 or 15 planes, and
crush 7 or 8 M. 113 amphibious carriers. If formerly we could
attack only suddenly to withdraw immediately, today we can fight
the whole day long under the fire power of the enemy artillery
and air force which drop hundreds of tons of bombs ; and if
formerly we could destroy only posts defended by 10 or 20
enemy troops. today our army can raze to the ground series
of posts and strongholds manned by hundreds of enemy troops.''

According to the figures given by Liberation Radio, due to the
foregoing growth of the South Vietnam people's armed forces,
during the three years of guerilla warfare (1961-1963) the South
Vietnam army and people destroyed and disbanded more than
250,000 enemy troops, including nearly 1,500 Americans downed
and damaged hundreds of enemy airplanes, captured over
30,000 weapons of all descriptions (in 1963 alone 80,000 enemy
troops were put out of action, 982 Americans killed, and 40,000
puppet troops disbanded).

At the end of 1963, the U.S. imperialists and their henchmen
recognized that 80 per cent of the 8,000 "strategic hamlets'' they
had established were completely destroyed by the people. The
rest exists only by name, the controlling machinery of the enemy
being complety crushed.

1964

January 1, 1964 : The Congress of the South Vietnam Liberation National Front opens ; it lasts until January 8. The
composition of the Front Central Committee is broader than
before. Lawyer Nguyen Huu Tho is elected President of the
Front. The Congress scores brilliant successes and unanimously
sanctions important resolutions with a view to bringing the
resistance for national salvation to victory. In the political report
delivered before the Congress, Lawyer Nguyen Huu Tho affirms
the optimistic confidence in the success of the resistance for
national salvation waged by the South Vietnamese people :

"The victories scored by the resistance war have a great significance and open a period full of promise. Never is the situation so bright as today".

January 4, 1964 : About the attitude of the United States toward the Duong Van Minh administration, Joseph Alsop writes in the New York Herald Tribune that those who analyse the former situation and clamour for the overthrow of Ngo Dinh Diem begin to complain that his successors, members of the Revolutionary Military Council in South Vietnam, are not worthy of U.S support.

January 17, 1964 . Biggest raid launched by the Americans and their lackeys against Thanh Phu (Ben Tre province, Nam Bo) after overthrowing Diem. According to American papers, in the records of helicopter tactics of the United States in South Vietnam, this is a battle where the largest number of helicopters is used. It is directed by the U.S. Military Command and the command of the puppet army in Saigon under the direction of an American lieutenant-general and 28 U.S. "advisers" together with Gen. Le Van Kim, Chief-of-Staff of the South Vietnam army, Le Van Phat, Commander of the Third tactical zone, etc. The raid lasts 20 days involving a force 5,000-strong, scores of warships, 26 amphibious armoured carriers M. 113, and 60 guns, but is completely defeated by the Liberation army and the local people ; 600 enemies including 10 U.S. officers and a British colonel, William Lee, Royal Air Force Commander, are annihilated, 32 planes of various types shot down or damaged, 2 boats and warships destroyed.

The Thanh Phu victory marks the first defeat of the U.S. aggressors' new military policy after the overthrow of Diem : reduction of posts, concentration of mobile forces, large-scale raids to annihilate the bulk of the South Vietnam people's armed force. After this victory the South Vietnam army and people win a series of resounding victories in 1964.

January 27, 1964 . At the meeting of the U.S. House Armed Forces Committee, McNamara declares that the "anti-communist" war in South Vietnam has taken a bad turn though Diem has been overthrown and the U.S.A. is ready to do everything to prevent the victory of the communists.

January 30, 1964: At 3.30 p.m. Gen. Nguyen Khanh, Commander of the Army Corps No. One of the South Vietnam puppet army, overthrows Duong Van Minh by a coup d'état. Some days later the new government of South Vietnam is set up with Nguyen Khanh as Premier and Nguyen Ton Hoan, a personality belonging to the Dai Viet Party, as Vice-Premier in charge of pacification. Duong Van Minh is the "President" by name.

U.P.I. reports that according to well-informed source Gen. Nguyen Khanh encouraged by his American collaborators in Army corps No. One engineers the coup d'état to "re-organize the Revolutionary Military Council" with a view to opposing the wave of neutratity. It also says that on the night of January 29, 1964, U S ambassador to Saigon, Cabot Lodge, has been informed of the coup d'etat On January 31, 1964, A.P. reports that U S. President Johnson has been kept informed of it and has closely followed the outcome of the event.

February 1, 1964 : As Chairman of the Revolutionary Military Council Nguyen Khanh promulgates Decree No. 93 outlawing the communists and neutralists.

February 13, 1964 : A.F.P. reports that after the conference between British Prime Minister Home and Johnson in the U.S.A. a joint communiqué has been issued mentioning among other things that Great Britain supports the U.S. policy in South Vietnam and the U.S A. supports her in the Malaysian problem.

February 21, 1964 : At Los Angeles when speaking of the situation in South Vietnam U.S. President Johnson declares. "Those engaged in external direction and support would do well to remember that this type of aggression is a deeply dangerous game". This declaration has paved the way for a propaganda in the American press "to carry the war to North Vietnam".

March 8, 1964 : McNamara comes to Saigon. U.P.I. reports that during his stay in South Vietnam, McNamara sanctions the plan of "pacification" worked out by the Nguyen Khanh clique and its U.S. "advisers". McNamara and Nguyen Khanh agree on the basic strategy pointed out in the plan, that is to concentrate regular units in the dangerous zones in order to help the military forces annihilate the guerillas during large-scale operations for pacification and to foster the semi-armed units to be used in the less dangerous zones.

March 12, 1964 . A.P. reports that Senator Wayne Morse of the Democrat Party demands the withdrawal of U.S. troops from South Vietnam. He opposes the participation of the U.S A. in the war in South Vietnam, and says that it has neither interests nor legal basis to participate in what he calls the civil war in South Vietnam.

March 27, 1964 · McNamara openly declares : "The U.S. did not rule out the possibility of carrying the war to North Vietnam."

March 27, 1964 : At the special political conference convened in Hanoi President Ho Chi Minh declares :
"At present the U S. bellicists and their new lackeys trumpet about "marching to the North" But they must understand that if they are rash enough to attack North Vietnam they will fail piteously because all our people will resist them energetically ; the socialist countries and the progressive peoples the world over will wholeheartedly support us, and the American people and the allies of the U.S.A will oppose them."

April 4, 1964 Nguyen Khanh signs an order to pressgang soldiers, including women.

April 13, 1964 : In an interview granted to Australian journalist Wilfred Burchett, Gen. Vo Nguyen Giap Minister of National Defence and Commander-in-Chief of the Vietnam People's Army, declares "Any aggression against the D.R.V. by the Americans and their lackeys will be an act of suicide".

April 15, 1964 : At the 10th session of the S.E.A.T.O. military bloc held in Manila (Philippines), the U.S.A. coerces a number of participating countries to issue a communiqué saying about

South Vietnam: "The Council agreed that the members of S.E.A.T.O. should remain prepared, if necessary, to take further concrete steps within their capabilities in fulfilment of their obligations under the treaty".

April 23, 1964: Speaking about South Vietnam U.S. President Johnson declares: "I would hope that we would see some other flags in there as a result of the S.E.A.T.O. meeting and other conferences we have had."

April 25, 1964: Johnson appoints Gen. Westmoreland commander of the Military Aid Command in Saigon in replacement of Gen. Harkins.

April 30, 1964. Nguyen Khanh promulgates law 10-64 to stifle freedom of speech.

May 2, 1964: South Vietnam Liberation troops sink the U.S. 15,000-ton aircraft carrier Card, killing and wounding 55 American aggressors, and sending 19 planes to the bottom of the Saigon river.

May 15, 1964. The Americans merge the Military Aid Advisory Group to the Military Aid Command in South Vietnam.

May 25, 1964: According to A.P. since the coming of Nguyen Khanh into office till May 1964 60 papers have been closed or suspended.

May 31, 1964: A.P. reports that Melvin Laird, member of the U.S. House of Representatives Defence Appropriations Committee, confirms that the Johnson administration's position is to march to the North, and many preparatory works for this task are carried on.

June 23, 1964: Gen. Maxwell Taylor is appointed U.S. ambassador to South Vietnam after the resignation of Cabot Lodge Alexis Johnson is appointed vice-ambassador.

August 2, 1964: The U.S. destroyer Maddox which violates the territorial waters of the D.R.V. and fires first at the North Vietnam's patrol-ships, is driven away by the latter.

August 4, 1964 : The Americans fabricate the so-called "second incident of North Vietnam Gulf" by saying that two U.S. destroyers, Maddox and Turner Joy, have been attacked by D R V. torpedo-boats in the international waters of the Gulf of North Vietnam.

August 5, 1964 · The U.S. planes bomb and strafe a number of localities of North Vietnam coastal region. The army and people of the D.R V. deal heavy blows at the enemy 8 planes are shot down and 3 others damaged, the flight lieutenant, Everett Alvarez Jr, is captured.

August 7, 1964 : Nguyen Khanh promulgates law 18-64, declares state of emergency and martial law all over South Vietnam. According to this law a series of fascist measures have been taken, such as house-to-house searches, prohibition of workers' strikes and market strikes, demonstrations ; censorship of the press, films, and printed material ; limitation of circulation, free requisition of the people's property ; act of "violation" to be summoned before a military court ; possibility of sentencing to death without trial, etc.

August 15, 1964 : Setting up of the joint Vietnam-U.S. Military Command. According to Reuter, with such a command, the Americans will have the same right as the Vietnamese in taking the decisions on tactics and are no longer advisers as before.

August 16, 1964 : Nguyen Khanh puts forth a "charter" and takes in hand all power, at the same time he names himself "President of the Republic of Vietnam", and kicks Duong Van Minh out of the "Presidency".

From August 17 to August 24, 1964 : With U.S. support Nguyen Khanh schemes to set up a personal military dictatorship ; students, pupils, Buddhists and other strata of the urban population in the South, especially in Hue and Saigon, step up a seething movement of fierce struggle for the abrogation of the "August 16, 1964 charter", the annulment of the order for the state of emergency and martial law, the overthrow of Nguyen

Khanh, the opposition to the U.S. imperialists' intervention in South Vietnam. These struggles draw tens of thousands of people, and are waged under the forms of meetings and demonstrations, including those demanding to meet Nguyen Khanh in person. On August 23, 600 Saigon students march to the Saigon boadcasting station and attack it because it distorts the result of this interview.

August 25, 1964: 30,000 people march to Nguyen Khanh's house in Saigon demanding to overthrow him and to abolish the regime of military dictatorship, and shouting anti-U.S. slogans; 20,000 people hold meetings at Ben Thanh market (Saigon), and about 40,000 Saigon people turn down the streets to back the struggle of the masses. The people of Da Nang town stage a general strike and market strike to protest against the U.S. aggressors who have fired at the demonstrators and caused a riot during which over 100 people were killed and wounded. In Hue the struggles intensify together with the mass demonstrations in Quy Nhon, Nha Trang, Quang Tri... In face of the wave of powerful struggle of the townspeople in South Vietnam Nguyen Khanh is obliged to make a declaration to dissolve the "Revolutionary Army Council'' and resign his post of "President of the Republic of Vietnam''.

Auguts 27, 1964: With a view to appeasing the struggle of the masses and after two days of hot discussion within and without the meeting hall, the so-called "Revolutionary Army Council'' in Saigon is obliged to declare :

— abrogation of the "August 16, 1964 charter'',

— dissolution of the "Revolutionary Army Council'',

— convening of the "National Congress" within two months to appoint the head of the U.S. sponsored puppet state machinery in South Vietnam,

— the founding of the so-called "provisional national and army steering committee'' comprising Duong Van Minh, Nguyen Khanh and Tran Thien Khiem, the three rival generals.

September 3, 1964: After five days of alleged convalescence at Dalat — in truth to shun the spearhead of the people's attack —

Nguyen Khanh is recalled by his American boss to Saigon and reinstated Prime minister. Since then he resolutely demoted his rivals and in fact the triumvirate within the provisional national and military steering committee is suppressed.

September 13, 1964 · Some general officers including Duong Van Duc, Lam Van Phat, Huynh Van Ton, Duong Hieu Nghia... brought troops into Saigon to overthrow Khanh. However, the coup does not last over 24 hours for the United States still supports Khanh. Though the latter is not overthrown the contradiction between the U.S. stooges in South Vietnam grows ever deeper, plunging the South Vietnam puppet administration into a serious crisis of disintegration.

September 18, 1964: The United States fabricates a new *"Tonkin Gulf incident"* but has to brush it away as the Government of the Democratic Republic of Vietnam timely exposes this deceptive move and world opinion vehemently condemn it. However, U S. imperialism and its lackeys has kept on creating tension, staging provocation and perpetrating war acts against the Democratic Republic of Vietnam.

September 20, 1964 The meeting of 500 officers and men from the Highlanders breaks out at Ban Me Thuot (Western Plateaux) to oppose the policy of repression by U.S. imperialism and its hirelings and to demand autonomy for the Western Plateaux nationalities · within a few days, the uprising spreads throughout Gia Lai and Dac Lac, involving 4,000 people; to crush this rebellion the U.S and Khanh use perfidious manœuvres along with military force.

September 21, 1964 50,000 workers and toiling people of Saigon-Cholon and Gia Dinh go on strike and demonstrate in support to the struggle of 1,800 workers of the Vimytex weaving-mill demanding that the 18-64 law by Nguyen Khanh which bans strikes and meetings by workers and toiling people be abrogated, democratic freedoms be ensured and jobs be given. For the first time, the Vietnamese working class displays its great force in strict discipline and order, paralysing all activities of the Saigon port.

September 26, 1964 : According to A.P. and U.P.I,, U.S. President Johnson officially discloses that U.S. planes have been allowed to penetrate into the air space of North Vietnam and People's Republic of China to pursue any Communist planes attacking U.S warships in the Tonkin Gulf.

*
* *

During the first nine months of 1964, in face of repeated setbacks of the U.S and its stooges in the "special war" raised to a high degree in South Vietnam, U.S. Defence Secretary McNamara twice visited Saigon (in March and May 1964) to study the situation The 13th (March) and 14th (June) Honolulu meetings were convened for this purpose. Present at the 14th meeting (June 1, 2, 1964) were 43 leading cadres in charge of foreign affairs, national defence and C.I.A. as well as U.S. ambassadors to Laos, South Vietnam and Thailand. According to Western reports, this meeting has discussed such problems as : to send U.S. troops to North Thailand near the Laotian border, to increase the most effective measures to step up the war of aggression against South Vietnam and to use planes to attack the supply routes of the "Viet Cong" and their nerve-centres outside the frontier of South Vietnam.

Up to mid-1964, the number of U.S. "advisors" and soldiers in South Vietnam amounted to more than 25,000 commanded by nearly 20 generals. According to U P I. of August 20, 1964 the United States would still introduce thousands of troops. Tne system of U.S. "advisers" tops the Ministry of National Defence down to battalions, and sometimes to companies. With the setting up of a joint Vietnam-U.S command in last August 1964, U.S. officers tighten their grip over the South Vietnam army. All important military bases throughout South Vietnam were occupied by U.S. troops. U S. means of war were increasingly introduced into South Vietnam and included a great quantity of up-to-date equipment. U S. military aid to South Vietnam in 1964 has reached 675 million dollars.

At present, by various expedients such as prolonging conscrip tion, calling reserve officers and men to the colours, launching raids to pressgang people, the southern administration has an army about 500,000 strong including regular, regional (formerly security guards) and militia (formerly village guards) troops.

The more it is defeated and bogged down in South Vietnam, the more the United States forces its hirelings frenziedly to step up their mopping-up operations and does not stop at any savage and inhuman act to massacre the people (wanton dropping of ton-bombs, napalm bombs, spraying of toxic chemicals etc.) These henchmen strive also to herd the popu- lation into "strategic hamlets" renamed "new-life hamlets".

*

Pushing ahead the movement of "Ap Bac emulation to kill the enemy and score feats of arms" launched by the South Vietnam Liberation National Front, over the first nine months of this year after the great victory against the U.S.-puppet large-scale raid at Thanh Phu (January 1964) the South Vietnam Liberation army and people smashed mopping-up operations and won many other great victories such as at Kontum, Hau My, Long Thuan, Ba Long, Binh Trung, Thuong Phuoc, Phu Le, Phu My, My Phuoc, Vinh Thuan, Mang Xinh, Bang Lang, Pleikrong, Nam Dong, Chanh Luu, Vuon Thom, Vinh Cheo, Binh Long, Cai Be, Go Quao, Phu Tuc, Vinh Phuoc, Phu Huu, Phu Cu, etc In each battle the enemy suffered casualties from 300 to 700 men, and lost more and more U.S. weapons. In several engagements the southern army and people wiped out hundreds of American aggressors such as the raid upon the headquarters of U.S. "advisors" at Kontum (February 2, 1964), those upon the Tan Son Nhat airfield and the Capitol Cinema (February 9 and 16, 1946) and the attack of the Caravelle Hotel in Saigon (August 25, 1964).

In the first half of 1964 the South Vietnam army and people :
-- fought the enemy in 14,000 battles,

— put out of action 71,000 enemy troops (wiped out and captured 42,000, among them 826 Americans ; 29,000 puppet troops crossed over to the people's side),

— seized 5,600 weapons of various kinds, millions of cartridges and grenades, hundreds of radio transmitters and many kinds of equipment,

— set aflame and destroyed 278 amphibious cars and military vehicles, sank and damaged 84 warships and motor boats among which the 15,000-ton aircraft carrier Card.

— shot down 170 planes of various types and damaged over 320 others,

— completely destroyed nearly 2,000 "strategic hamlets" and extended the liberated areas in many regions.

In the political struggle, a movement surged from countryside to town ; the southern people successively launched fierce and repeated political offensives against the U.S. aggressors and the Nguyen Khanh clique to oppose their policy of ruthless oppression and their savage terrorist raids by bombs, bullets and toxic chemicals. According to still incomplete figures, in the first half of 1964 alone, a total of 12 million people was recorded for having participated in meetings and demonstrations against the U.S.-puppets.

In face of the repeated victories of the South Vietnam people the U.S.-puppet plan of "pacifying" South Vietnam has obviously shrunk : if while early in 1962 Harkins planned to "pacify" 10 provinces in the Mekong delta, in March 1964 McNamara when visiting Saigon brought the number down to 7 provinces around Saigon and Quang Ngai province in Trung Bo. However, in June 1964, when assuming the post of "ambassador" Taylor reduced it to three provinces : Long An, Thu Dau Mot, Go Cong, and four districts Duc Hoa, Duc Hue, Cu Chi and Trang Bang. And in October 1964 the "pacification" plan was again curtailed to only some districts around Saigon.

The resistance for national salvation of the South Vietnam people has constantly developed and scored victory after victory, and the position of the South Vietnam Liberation National Front has ever been raised in the world arena . up to mid-1964, 32 delegations of the Front and patriotic organizations within it have visited 19 countries in Europe, Asia, Africa and Latin America, 10 international organizations have affiliated the Front and the patriotic organizations within it ; besides the Front has sent delegations to 31 conferences convened by various international organizations and the delegates of the National Liberation Front have been elected Executive Committee members of 6 international organizations.

October 1964

Printed in the United Kingdom by
Lightning Source UK Ltd., Milton Keynes
139115UK00001B/9/A